D1446603

THE
LITTLE CHILDREN
AND OTHER OBSERVATIONS

THE
LITTLE CHILDREN
AND OTHER OBSERVATIONS

W. ROD OLSON

Halo
PUBLISHING
INTERNATIONAL

Copyright © 2023 W. Rod Olson All rights reserved.

No part of this publication may be reproduced, stored in a retrieval system or transmitted in any form or by any means, electronic, mechanical, photocopying, recording or otherwise, without prior permission of Halo Publishing International.

The views and opinions expressed in this book are those of the author and do not necessarily reflect the official policy or position of Halo Publishing International. Any content provided by our authors are of their opinion and are not intended to malign any religion, ethnic group, club, organization, company, individual or anyone or anything.

For permission requests, write to the publisher, addressed "Attention: Permissions Coordinator," at the address below.

Halo Publishing International
7550 WIH-10 #800, PMB 2069,
San Antonio, TX 78229

First Edition, June 2023
ISBN: 978-1-63765-410-1
Library of Congress Control Number: 2023907096

The information contained within this book is strictly for informational purposes. Unless otherwise indicated, all the names, characters, businesses, places, events and incidents in this book are either the product of the author's imagination or used in a fictitious manner. Any resemblance to actual persons, living or dead, or actual events is purely coincidental.

Halo Publishing International is a self-publishing company that publishes adult fiction and non-fiction, children's literature, self-help, spiritual, and faith-based books. We continually strive to help authors reach their publishing goals and provide many different services that help them do so. We do not publish books that are deemed to be politically, religiously, or socially disrespectful, or books that are sexually provocative, including erotica. Halo reserves the right to refuse publication of any manuscript if it is deemed not to be in line with our principles. Do you have a book idea you would like us to consider publishing? Please visit www.halopublishing.com for more information.

To my parents,
Mary Lou Bernini Olson
and William Nathaniel Olson.

Both highly accomplished in their own lives,
they continue to be my inspiration,
my North Star.

Contents

The Little Children

I had a moment yesterday, a reality check, when the images on television were suddenly live and in front of me. I have the good fortune of working with a client in Mexico City two weeks each month. I am staying at a nice hotel on the Paseo de la Reforma, which was constructed in the 1800s by Maximilian I, when France ruled this area. Maximilian was trying to modernize Mexico City, as Napoleon III was doing in Paris. The Paseo is modeled after the Champs Elysée; it exhibits quite a bit of wealth, as the Champs Elysée does. The people here are wonderfully friendly and helpful.

I was working from my hotel room when my computer mouse gave out, forcing me to walk to a nearby office supply store to buy a new one. On the way down Paseo de la Reforma, I passed a young girl, about eight or nine, with a toddler running around her. The young girl was seated on the sidewalk, leaning against a building. Life hadn't been so good for them, from their appearances. The young girl was a sweet little lady with a broad smile and a twinkle in her young eyes. She gently offered her begging cup to me with that big smile and her sparkling eyes quite wide.

I found myself not wondering how those kids got there or why they were there. The relevant fact for me was that they were there at all. I wanted to scoop them up and take them home with me if I could—take them off the street, feed them, dress them, and educate them.

As a world, we have much to do to help our fellow inhabitants of this Earth. Shouldn't we take care of our fellow people first? Isn't this our mission here on Earth? Yes, I've seen those begging on the streets of Manhattan, but never have I seen a child, alone, doing so. Sometimes I forget, living in the comfort of my home, what the reality of life is for kids in need, such as these two sweet little ones on the Paseo de la Reforma.

Speaking French in Mexico

I am back in Mexico City for two weeks, on-site at my client's office.

Yesterday, I stopped at a Starbucks. I fumbled through another attempt at ordering in Spanish, and finally said, *"No habla Español,"* which in itself was incorrect.

The barista of early college age replied, *"Parlez-vous français?"*

Okay, I was stopped in my tracks; I paused and gave thought to his reply. I then said that I only spoke English.

In English, the young man said that he thought I may be French. He spoke three languages.

Almost everyone with whom I work in Mexico City speaks both English and Spanish. I found this to be the same when having the good fortune of working in Madrid years ago. I have repeatedly said that I wish our educational systems in the United States required conversational proficiency in a second language. And I wish I had given more effort to my French classes with Mrs. Nichols in high school. But I didn't.

So as I thought through my encounter with the young Mexican barista who spoke Spanish, French, and English, I thought, too, about the educational systems in the United States. Why as a country do we give such high importance to the need to fund our crumbling infrastructure of bridges and roads, when an equally, if not more, important source of funding is needed for the infrastructure that comprises our educational systems? What about the young minds needing to be educated in order to maintain the crumbling bridges and roads while competing in an increasingly shrinking global marketplace? What about all the other countries that require second-language education? Can we compete?

And then I thought about my cousin Barb, a lifelong educator whose parents and sister were also educators. And I thought about my college friend Louise who was president of her university's senior class and whose education career led her to an appointment as a principal in her school district. And I thought about one of my best friends from childhood, Garry, and my friends Jessie, Beth, Katrina, and Dan, all of whom are accomplished, lifelong educators. I recall conversations with them about the lack of supplies and support while they were teaching. I often wondered why educators are paid less than engineers. Aren't they engineering minds? What's more important? A bridge or a mind?

Then there is my friend Cindy who took over as the kindergarten teacher in the school district of my youth when Mrs. George, my kindergarten teacher, retired. As a consultant, I often start new-client meetings with an icebreaker: I ask everyone in the room to name their favorite teacher and explain why they were the favorite. EVERYONE always is quick with an answer. Amazing. People can recall teachers from their distant past, but can't recall what they may have worn yesterday.

Just some thoughts…after all, Starbucks in Mexico City has baristas who speak three languages…

Words

I am in Mexico City again, working with a client.

One morning last week, I sat having breakfast and listening/watching the Mexican national news on the television in front of me. The top-three stories were centered on the events of this past week in the United States. The images weren't pretty, and while only comprehending some of what the news anchors were saying, I found myself feeling as if I were a kid whose parents just had a horrific argument that somehow the whole neighborhood knew about; my neighborhood friends were looking at me differently, but not saying a word. I am sure that my childhood-neighborhood friend Joni may have felt this on her recent trip to Cuba, or another childhood friend Bev on her recent trip to South America, or another childhood friend Jessie while living in India and China.

Others know what is going on inside my home.

Words and images are powerful. They are the principal source of communication. When the words aren't fully comprehended, and you only have images to understand the situations in front of you, your comprehension suddenly is more penetrating and more powerful…and can be more frightening.

I returned to my hotel one night last week after a more challenging day at the office, had dinner, and sat down to watch television to relax. I was bombarded with more events from the United States. I turned off the television, and as I did, the opening line of the poem "Desiderata"—the Latin word meaning desired things—by Max Ehrmann, written in 1927, popped into my head: "Go placidly among the noise and the haste, and remember what peace there may be in silence." I Googled the poem and read it. It provided a grounding and a centering.

I first became acquainted with this poem my junior year in college. I found a poster of it in Spencer Gifts, bought it, and hung it above my college-dorm bed. As an aside, my roommate, Bill, had the iconic Farah Fawcett poster above his bed.

Over the years, "Desiderata" has resurfaced again and again in my brain.

It is interesting how the mind works...

Pinpoints of Light

I am at home now from my work in Mexico City. It is Christmas Eve.

It is good to be home after wishing all my colleagues at my client's office in Mexico City, "*Feliz Navidad y Próspero Año Nuevo.*" I bid the same to all my friends who work at the hotel in which I am almost a resident now. I gave a hug to the housekeeper who manages my room each day; she hugged back. It is acceptable to hug in Mexico City. She is a special person with a very sweet personality and big smile. Neither of us speak each other's native language, but we still do communicate quite clearly with each other. It is amazing what smiles can communicate.

I've come to understand that it is the moments in life that stay with us, not the events. In checking LinkedIn, one of my college friends posted a message to me that his father passed away. I knew that his father had been ill and that my friend, after working through his own heart's bypass surgery, was his dad's caregiver. But of the three years living next to my friend while in college, the moment that came back to me when I read this news was of my friend, returning from a final exam when we were in college, sitting down on my dorm-room bed, and suddenly falling asleep, exhausted from studying and the stress of the test. I was sitting on my roommate's bed, studying, when he came into our room. I let him sleep. I understood that feeling of being totally spent from studying. For some reason, that moment has lived with me.

Once, when it seemed as if all my nine aunts' and uncles' families were gathered at Grandma Olson's house for a summer event that included homemade vanilla ice cream, the oldest of my eventually eighteen Olson first cousins enthusiastically went to her parents' car, brought out a badminton set, threw up the net, and then corralled us older cousins into a game. I was number six in the line down in age from the eldest, and in front of me were two future cheerleaders, one high school basketball star and prom king, one homecoming queen, and one beauty queen.

I was terrified, as my eye-hand coordination wasn't well-developed yet, and the idea of being the worst of my cousins at badminton was overwhelming. But my eldest cousin's enthusiasm that day is still burned into my brain. I still see and feel the moment she brought us together for that game as if it were yesterday in front of Grandma's home.

And during Christmases, my family visited with the family of my friend Rita. Rita's parents, Joe (a.k.a. Punchy) and Irene, had a Nativity scene under their Christmas tree each year. I still remember that setting. The gifts all around it and the games I probably played with Rita and Gene, her brother, are memories that are no longer in the forefront of my brain. The Nativity scene is, however. It may have been the reason my mother bought our Nativity scene, which is now sitting in my home. It reminds me not only of Christmases with my family, but also of that one Christmas at the Grassonis' when their Nativity scene took a special place in my mind.

I had news yesterday of several life-defining moments. I guess it is these moments that pick a spot in our brains and stay there, small pinpoints of light that blink through at certain times. These blinks are clearly meaningful and meant to be there. I don't think we ever realize that our brains are registering these life-defining moments when they occur. But I find it interesting that our brains spark a memory just when we may need a bit of comfort or a smile.

A few years ago, I was trading Christmas memories with a work colleague. She wrote that Christmas is her favorite time of the year. She went on to say that for her country of birth, her memory was of the last year of Soviet occupation. Christmas wasn't openly celebrated, but those who quietly did put a candle in their window as a silent protest against the regime. At 9:00 p.m. on Christmas Eve that year, she remembers standing with her mother at a window of their home and seeing every single neighborhood window with a lit candle. It is a picture she said she can still see when she closes her eyes. Another moment for her, and for me, as her email message is still vivid in my brain. This memory makes me often think of what it would be like if I could not celebrate Christmas openly. I keep a copy of her email among the pages of Luke 2.

What is it in us that allows these pinpoints of light in our memories to flicker more brightly or shine like a beacon at certain times in life? I am glad they are there, providing comfort when needed and a smile that only each of us, within our own minds, can fully understand. And I am grateful they are there, waiting to shine through.

Millennials

So…I read a lot about millennials, and I have been working with a lot of them. I honestly can't remember all the labels given to the latest generations and often need to refer to a crib sheet I made for myself to remember them. I know I am a baby boomer…born in the middle of the baby boom after World War II. I remember this label from years ago. We were, and are still, considered a special breed, born to the Greatest Generation after World War II.

Next came Generation X, or Gen Xers, as they are more commonly known, born between 1965 and 1980. I am not sure when the label was given to them, but I do recall it suddenly prominently emerging in the media in the 1990s. And then came the infamous millennials, born between 1981 and 1996. We hear them referred to a lot now in the media and in conversation. And, finally, there is Generation Z, or Gen Zers, the tots among all our labeled generations, born between 1997 and some year to be designated at a later point in time by the people who officially name generations.

I read about the concerns millennials have and the work they are doing to address their concerns. I think there was some crossover from millennials to Gen Z as the Gen Zers entered their twenties. Some ideas of the millennials seem needed, some are needed, some seem radical, some have far-reaching implications, and some are for immediate needs. None seems to be much different than my generation had at that age. Millennials are different, though, from my generation. They do have a different work ethic.

I also read that they like experiences, but I am not sure what that means. I did too at their age, and still do. Maybe my "experiences" were different, but they were experiences to me and still are. Maybe the difference now is that they are not a driving force in my life, as perhaps they are for millennials.

In my first real job, I remember a vice president of strategic research, a man in his sixties, once telling me, "Spend all your money on yourself in your twenties, and then start saving in your thirties. Your twenties only come once, and there is plenty of time to settle down." He went on to say, and I paraphrase again, "You will see that you will begin to think differently when you reach your thirties."

I took his advice. I "experienced."

While I am definitely a boomer, I am also a product of the late 1960s and the Me Generation of the 1970s. I came into full adulthood in the go-go eighties and watched the economy crash twice, once in 1987 and again in 2008. I remember my dad once asking me if I was a yuppie.

I cannot help but wonder if the millennial movement is like the baby-boomer movement of the 1960s—about peace and love, civil rights, and women's rights. I was still young in the 1960s, but old enough to understand what was happening. The sixties' generation basically said, "We've had enough. It is not working." Their parents' generation was a time of great strides, but unfortunately also a time of great distress, with the moon landing and the Vietnam War, with an overheated economy and striking poverty, with young leadership and old guards, with the progress of the Civil Rights Movement and the devastation of assassinations, with expanding technology and a world filling with pollution (the first Earth Day was in 1971).

For all the progress made by their parents, the sixties generation saw something much different: A world they were inheriting that they did not universally like. For me, the iconic song from that period, as it neared its end, may have been the New Seekers' "I'd Like to Teach the World to Sing," which was released in 1971.

I remember well how my parents' generation spoke of the hippies and yippies; and peace marches, draft dodgers, and draft-card burners; and Haight-Ashbury and free love. It wasn't nice. But maybe what they failed to see was the evolution of society, technology, and the world. Maybe what they failed to see was the foundations they gave to their children of the sixties generation taking root and producing strides, but perhaps not the strides they desired.

The parents of boomers came through the Great Depression when, for many, problems with providing daily food for their families and keeping roofs over their heads were constantly looming. They were then thrust into World War II due to the failings of the negotiated peace of World War I. This generation probably wasn't happy with their parents' generation, either, for their failures that put their children into a real line of fire.

Turn the page, and they were living the good life post-World War II as employment and wages soared for many, home ownership was a reality, and they were able to give their kids a life about which they'd only dreamed. The parents of boomers went on to try to win a war in Vietnam that wasn't winnable. Their kids only saw their friends dying in what seemed to be an endless war, not enough being done to stop it: The sixties generation was ignited.

Fast forward to the millennials, and despite all the opportunities provided to them by their parents' generation, two market crashes later, a warming Earth with its melting glaciers and rising seas, inequality, and a host of isms, and not enough being done to stop any of this—the millennial generation was ignited.

So, perhaps, what we are seeing with the millennials today is another generation saying, "We've had enough. It is not working." Maybe, like the boomers, they don't want to inherit the world as it is evolving. I seem to see a lot of similarities from a 50,000-foot view just fifty years later. A new chapter, but the same story: a shoving of the nimble, innovative youth against a bulwark of old.

The boomers protested and had sit-ins, love-ins, and walk-outs. Together with a lot of other classmates in my high school, I walked out of it one day in protest over something—I think it was the Vietnam War. The husband of one cousin and two of my next-door neighbors were in this war. One neighbor was killed; the other never spoke of it…or, perhaps, as a young male, I was too afraid of the answers if I questioned him about it. Of course, I walked out of school with the fear of my dad's finding out and my still being locked in my bedroom to this day for doing such a crazy thing.

But was it a crazy thing? The boomers did move the needle. Maybe not enough and maybe not in all the right directions, but they moved it. Maybe the millennials are moving it again. They seem to have reason to do so, just as the sixties generation did. Like it or not, we are passing the baton to them. Should we not embrace their youth, energy, innovative thinking, and experience-based lives and try to guide them as they evolve, rather than question it?

Chance Meetings?

We all have those moments when a song from your past pops into your head, and suddenly you are humming it while trying to piece the lyrics together while tapping your foot.

I am back in Mexico City. Last night, after an intense day of work for my client in my hotel room, I retired to a long-awaited, relaxing dinner. Sitting alone in a restaurant, I found Alicia Keys's "We Are Here" going around in my brain. I finally gave up and did a search on my cell phone to find it on YouTube. While staring at the video, completely engrossed in trying to decipher all the lyrics, the restaurant's sound system was blaring a disco beat in the background. The waiter delivered my order; he then poured a dressing over it, even though I had stated when I ordered that I did not want any dressing. However, I hadn't been paying attention because Alicia's song had ahold of me. I sent the dish back for a redo.

I first heard "We Are Here" performed at Middle Collegiate Church in New York City. (Yes, I don't follow popular music any longer.) The song struck me, and after church, I called my cousin Linda to ask her if she had heard it. She had and, like me, was struck by the lyrics.

Linda moved on to her next life a few years ago after a noble and hard-fought battle with breast cancer. We were like brother and sister. In her eulogy, I stated, "We were cousins by birth, best friends by choice." I thought of her again last night as I listened to Alicia. I continue to feel as if Linda were just a phone call away.

It is funny how music and memories connect with each other. Music can whisk us away to another moment in time, another person, another feeling. Funny, too, how some music strikes deep in our hearts and deep in our souls. I am not the first to reflect on this…

The lyrics to "We Are Here" are worth taking time to digest. The line about souls brought together strikes me the most. I often say that we are all on this Earth together. This leads me to think…of all the people I have been fortunate to meet in life, were they really chance meetings?

Or is there a greater purpose?

Liza

On a recent Saturday morning, I was listening to "Paint the Sky with Stars" on *The Best of Enya*. Saturday-morning music decisions usually set the tone for my day. Often-times, they are chosen with much deliberation; sometimes, they are chosen simply on a whim. The choice of Enya followed a particularly busy week of work. I needed "slow down" music.

Enya's song, "Orinoco Flow" has been a favorite of mine since I first heard it on the second floor of the Liz Claiborne store on Fifth Avenue in New York City. I was head of planning and allocation for Liz Claiborne Retail then, and I was in the store for my periodic assessment of inventory levels on a Saturday morning. I asked Ramona, the second-floor manager, as she stood behind the cash wrap across from the denim wall, what the name of the song was.

Jim was our president of Liz Claiborne Retail then, and Ed was vice president of stores. Maria was head of merchandising for Liz Claiborne, and Olivia was head of merchandising for Elisabeth (plus sizes). Rounding out our team was Robin as vice president of marketing and my now longtime business partner, Kim, was the merchandise controller. It was a special time for us. We had a synergy that colleagues in a business environment seldom experience. While every day was not perfect and we did have our challenges, we were a team; we knew it and felt it and supported each other through our ride there.

We had a few bumps along the road, however. One of the most notable was when corporate at Liz Claiborne moved our offices from the convenience of New York City (where most of us lived) to Secaucus, New Jersey. And once we ran out of yellow printer ink at 2:00 a.m. the morning before a strategic meeting with the CEO of Liz, requiring us to drop the presentation at a FedEx office at 4:00 a.m. to have copies printed; then all of us rushing home to sleep for one hour before showering, suiting up, and picking up the presentation from the FedEx office before our meeting at 9:00 a.m. that day. We were a team.

One morning around 8:00 a.m., Ed was conducting a meeting with all of us on the first floor of the Liz Claiborne store on Fifth Avenue. During the meeting, we suddenly heard a *tap, tap, tap* on the windows facing Fifth Avenue. It was Liza Minnelli. She was holding a small, fluffy white dog. She motioned to us that she wanted to come into the store. Signaling with his hands, Ed directed Liza to the employee entrance, as the store was not open to the public at that time of the morning.

Suddenly, there she was....in front of all of us...Liza.

Liza explained that she was looking for a dress to wear that evening to an event, which was to be televised.

Our business meeting became insignificant at that moment; it ended quickly as we all scrambled to assist with Ms. Minnelli's wardrobing needs. I think it was Maria who sent me to the stockroom to find every size-six black dress that we owned. Ms. Minnelli bought a dress that became a bestseller after she was seen in it on television that night.

What does this boy from Black Lick, Pennsylvania, remember most about that morning with Liza Minelli in the Liz Claiborne store on Fifth Avenue in New York City? How nice she was. How genuine. Yes, how nice and how genuine with all of us.

Italian Markets

So the family-operated Italian market in my neighborhood closed this past week after 102 years in business, a victim of two large chain grocery stores opening nearby. For those of you who aren't familiar with New York City, the city is made up of multiple residential neighborhoods where you stop and talk to friends and acquaintances on the streets and where local shop owners know your name and you know theirs. For my local Italian market, there was the vivacious Vivian at checkout; Peter, Bruno, and Hugo at the prepared-foods counters; and Mike and Angel at the fresh meats, fish, and cheese counters. During the last week of operations, the owners posted a signboard with all the employees' names and their years of service. Many had been employed over ten years with the company. This said something.

Growing up, my family, together with Aunt Della, Uncle Mario, and Cousin Marla, made semiannual trips to Greensburg, Pennsylvania, to an Italian market, the interior of which had aromas that are still vivid in my sense memories. My mom was first-generation Italian, so we stocked up on a lot of Italian specialties, the likes of which would now be served with sides of cholesterol medication.

One of the semiannual trips was to buy the ingredients for ravioli and pasta. We had a kitchen in the 1960s base-ment-turned-family room of our home; there, at least once a year, Mom, Aunt Della, Aunt Nellie, and Aunt Dolly spent the weekend making 1,500 to 2,000 ravioli, followed by noodles, rows and rows of which were dried on lines hung in another area of the basement. Sometimes, Aunt Giggi and Aunt Marian would join them.

Day one was prep; day two was production. They all wore aprons, and flour was everywhere. They laughed, joked, and retold the same stories each year, enjoying the memories of their childhood and teenage years. My cousin Marla and I would eat a few raw ravioli, after which we were always told that we would get sick if we ate too many.

Partway through day two, Aunt Dolly went upstairs to the main kitchen and began making broth for the ravioli. Around 5:00 p.m. or so, my uncles arrived, and we all ate. The remaining ravioli were dried, bagged, and distrib-uted among the sisters and sisters-in-law in anticipation of Christmas or Easter dinners.

An Italian market was always part of my life. It must be in my DNA. My former neighborhood market was the place to stop when you didn't feel up to cooking dinner. The prepared-foods selections were fresh each day and only required reheating. Lunchtime offered a wide array of sandwiches, and if you didn't find what you wanted, they would make it.

Now, it is gone. Over recent years, the owners tried hard to compete with the grocery chains. But with time, the specialty foods and grocery selections straight from Italy gave way to products with mass-market names in their efforts to compete with the larger grocery stores nearby. The meat and cheese cases became more generic. I sensed that Peter, the grandson of one of the owners, was no longer making early morning trips to Fulton Fish Market to buy their legendary fresh seafoods for his daily selections. Several years ago, the owners closed one-half of the store and converted it to a wine bar with light fare. In doing so, most of the specialty foods and pasta selections from Italy disappeared.

I wonder why my neighborhood Italian market lost its appeal? When the big grocery stores opened, my Italian market still carried their specialties that set them apart from the chains. But, clearly, they began losing their customer base. Is it that my neighborhood suddenly didn't appreciate good, homemade Italian foods any longer? Or are we, as a culture, becoming accustomed to mass-market products purchased in massive, homogenous-looking grocery-store chains in which fish is labeled "Previously Frozen," and meats and chicken are conspicuously pumped up with some type of liquid, packed in Styrofoam trays, and labeled "No Antibiotics"? Or is it that low prices, plastic packaging, and mass production now, in importance, outweigh taste, personal service, and being greeted by name?

I will miss having my fish and meat cut to order. I will miss someone behind the cheese counter making a recommendation. I will miss the terrines and pâtés purchased not only to impress friends and family, but also to elevate the palate of this boy from Black Lick, Pennsylvania. Most of all, I will miss the people. Peter, the grandson, thanked me for many years of loyalty and told me that I was one of the few customers who never complained. I guess he forgot that one Thanksgiving when my special-order Thanksgiving dinner for four was missing the pint of spiced pecan-cranberry sauce. I decided to not remind him of the scene.

So life moves forward. Jennifer, a cashier whom I got to know at one of the big grocery chains, recently showed me her engagement ring and told me about the surprise event. She couldn't wipe the smile off her face. I was genuinely happy for her, and perhaps someday I will know her as I knew Vivian, Peter, Angel, Mike, Hugo, and Bruno. But my cart of big-chain products can't replace the fresh produce and the French-roasted chicken from my former neighborhood Italian market. Fortunately, I have my sense memories of my time there.

School

Someone once told me your closest friendships emerge from college since you suffered together. I can attest to this, but will add that we suffered together while emerging into adulthood and listening to Boston and Springsteen. But I have been thinking about the bonds from our elementary and high school days. They are a different type of bond, perhaps because they originated in childhood innocence from our first years together in school; maybe they are not always as deep, but there is a thread of connection that remains throughout life. What is that thread that starts to form in kindergarten and persists as we mature?

The theme from the movie *The Sting* has been swirling around in my head this morning. My classmate Wendy played it during her piano performance at our high school graduation. What happened over the thirteen years from kindergarten to senior year was a whirlwind when I think back on those years, but an eternity while going through them. Remember those summer breaks that never seemed to arrive, and then never seemed to end? All those fresh, young, and very cute faces on our kindergarten composite photos evolved into those "ready for life" graduation photos in our yearbook. Well, we thought we were ready for life as we lockstepped into the Blairsville Senior

High School gymnasium, donned in caps and gowns and excited to move that tassel to the other side of our mortarboards.

As a rite of passage, once upon a time, the Burrell Township grade-school kids and the Blairsville grade-school kids in sixth grade would merge into Blairsville Junior High School. Some would now call it a middle school; we knew it as junior high. It sounded more grown-up. The school itself was in Blairsville and was the former high school that many of our parents attended; it had a façade and the character of wholesomeness right out of the 1946 movie *My Little Margie*. We Burrell kids, though, had to ride a bus to Blairsville—another rite of passage and one more thing to do in the morning, just as sleep was becoming ever more important and ever harder to emerge from each morning.

Junior high meant having a homeroom and changing classes among a myriad of teachers, all with different personalities and expectations. Our math teacher posted the sign Silence is Golden above the blackboard in her classroom. No need to guess what her expectations were. On my first day, another teacher told me she "wasn't going to put up with me exhibiting the same behavior as my mother exhibited during class." Hmmm…

With all the strangeness and the efforts to make new friends, gym was perhaps the height of jolting experiences. Boys had to wear kelly-green trunks; girls were kept separate from the boys and had to wear some pinkish-colored, one-piece uniform. It wasn't bad enough that our bodies were beginning the growing pains of adolescence. We were forced to compound this with calisthenics, which only aggravated the pain. How many of us ran home to sleep after school on days we had gym? And how many remember looking up at that rope that went to the ceiling of the gym and knowing that we were expected to climb it? And then, having done so, how many remember looking down, feeling like a cat in a tree, and wondering, "How will I get down?"

I remember learning the song "Blowing in the Wind" in junior-high chorus. In retrospect, this was quite progressive for a school during the height of the Vietnam War. We sang our hearts out, for sure, not knowing fully what we were saying, while each night at home the ravages of the war were seen on our black-and-white televisions. As junior high evolved into senior high for us, the meaning of the words became too clear and the meaning behind them too frightening. Most of us guys were staring the draft in the face, and we could see our future selves in the television images.

I took Fay to the junior prom. I, just as so many other sixteen-year-old males going to their first prom, was given a swatch of her blue prom gown so that I could match my shirt to it. I rented my tux from Waxler's Men's Store in Indiana. Upon picking it up the day of the prom, my perfectly matched blue shirt with the ruffles was two sizes too large, and there were no alternatives.

Mom pinned it down the back and pinned the sleeves so that it fit. I now wonder what Mom was thinking as she pinned the prom shirt of her once little boy.

I never took my jacket off that night, Fay, and that is why. I thought you should know after all these years. And you were very pretty that night! I remember that vividly.

Mr. Mruk taught my childhood friend Nancy and me to play the saxophone. I chose the sax because in fourth grade, while standing in line to choose an instrument, I heard Nancy say, "Saxophone." So I did the same. Yep. No thought. Just an echo. Nancy chose it because her older brother played it. Another thread connecting Nancy and me (in third grade we wrote poetry together).

I didn't know at the time, but my uncle Mario, when in his twenties, was a semiprofessional saxophonist who played in local swing bands. So, thanks to Nancy, another thread connecting Uncle Mario and me. Thank you, Nancy. I still love saxophone music.

I took Chrissy to see *The Poseidon Adventure* when we were sixteen. It was after returning home from a Forensic Speech and Debate competition. My mom and dad both agreed this was a good decision because "Chrissy came from a good family." I just thought she was cute. My dad gave me twenty dollars for the evening. Yes, and that covered the movie tickets and a quick bite at McDonald's afterwards.

Grandma Olson was happy with Leda, my date for the Freshman-Sophomore Hop, because she, too, came from a very good family and one that Grandma knew. Again, I just thought she was cute. Leda and I had a great time. Buying her wrist corsage of blue-tinted daisies was a father-son moment for me; my dad took me to pick it up at the florist, all the while giving me advice on how to conduct myself as a gentleman with Leda.

I really don't remember a lot from high school, though, other than studying. There was the frog I dissected and then reconstructed its skeleton during senior biology class. I took it home, only to receive a quizzical look from my mom as I proudly showed it to her. She permitted me to keep it on my bedroom dresser.

There was French class that, today, I deeply regret not taking more seriously. Mrs. Nichol, please note, after years of additional French classes for which I paid, I still can't converse in French, but I can hear you say, "*Répète après moi!*"

There was Mr. Seylor's American literature course during our junior year; that's when my love of reading was sparked. Our first novel, John Knowles's *A Separate Peace*, was that igniter. Mr. Seylor taught us the term "doppelgänger" in reference to Phineas, one of the two main characters, a term I have only heard once since then.

And there was our calculus and trigonometry teacher, Mr. Kelly, to whom we dedicated our senior yearbook. As business manager for the yearbook, I remember the excitement the editors Connie, Sharene, and Donna shared when we received permission to reprint the song "When I'm Sixty-Four" on the dedication page to him. He was sixty-four when he retired. I am sorry to say I don't remember what trigonometry is. But I do remember that for Chas, Dave, and Connie, trig seemed to be strikingly easy.

Somehow, for some reason, the connection thread and memories to the people with whom we go through the first thirteen years of education remain. It is somewhere between acquaintance and sibling, undulating during that time and afterwards, maybe fading, maybe strengthening. Perhaps the connections are simply because we were in line formations many times during grade school, shoulder to shoulder in gym class, in alphabetical order for years of multiple homeroom assignments, one seat over or next to each other for thirteen long, formative years. Maybe we all experienced the biological phenomenon of horizontal gene transfer to a small degree during that time. Yes, maybe that is the reason.

Mother's Day

I am back in Mexico City this week. People here in Mexico City all seem to take their lunch hour, not unlike the two-hour lunches taken in Madrid, when my business partner, Kim, and I were working there.

The office of my client, El Palacio de Hierro, Mexico's largest luxury department store, really does clear at 2:00 p.m., and local restaurants fill to capacity. Reservations are often needed. And I am not talking fast-food lunches. Being the United States citizen that I am, I am always amazed at their devotion to this hour and tend to feel guilty taking a full hour for lunch.

Yesterday, Friday, May 10, was Mother's Day in Mexico. I ran down to the selling floors of Palacio to visit one of their in-house Starbucks in order to grab a quick sandwich, which I attempted to choke down, as usual, in record time so as not to miss a minute at my desk. "Very American," as they say here.

As I was sitting, devouring that sandwich at Starbucks, I witnessed many mothers walking arm in arm with their sons: teenage sons, twenty-, thirty-, and forty-year-olds, and older. It caused me to pause during my fifteen-minute lunch and observe. And smile. The scene took me back to

Sundays in Madrid when starting around eleven in the morning, as churches were ending their services, my business partner, Kim, and I would see entire families dressed in their Sunday finest, strolling the streets with baby carriages, toddlers, teenagers, moms and dads, grandparents, and aunts and uncles. Many were arm in arm, leisurely walking down the streets, engaging in conversations, laughing, and enjoying the moment with loved ones. No one seemed to be racing to get somewhere.

I have most of my dinners at Alfredo, an Italian restaurant in my hotel in Mexico City. Alfredo di Lelio, the founder of Alfredo, created fettuccine Alfredo, Alfredo's signature dish, in Rome around 1907 to 1908. He made the dish (without cream, by the way) to entice his wife to eat after giving birth to their first son. She liked it so much that he put it on the menu of his restaurant. A couple from the United States tried it and returned the following year to his restaurant with a set of gold spoons as a thank-you to Alfredo for this amazing pasta dish. Gold spoons are now always used in the restaurant to serve fettuccine Alfredo.

Alfredo last night was abuzz with Mother's Day celebrations. Cristian and Ivan, recently promoted from table attendants to waiters, were now donning the signature white jackets indicative of their promotions. I noticed that their gaits had changed as they maneuvered through the tables, from the rush of a busboy, to the stride of a professional. I was very happy for them. Cristian stopped at my table to show me his jacket.

While dining alone, I realized that I was now an observer of the activities of the tables around me on Mother's Day, and not a participant. Mothers were everywhere. As my eyes moved from table to table, I noticed something about the eyes of the mothers—looks of satisfaction, pride, admiration, care, hope, interest, and deep love, the kind of love that can only be felt, as words cannot harness it. Their gazes across the table—from son to daughter, grandson to granddaughter—moved slowly and methodically, hanging on every word and every action. I won't use the word "success" in what I observed. Their gazes seemed to know that their family was still evolving. Perhaps success is felt on the last day of life.

Behind me were two British gentlemen engaged in work-related conversation. Their British accents rose above the Spanish around me. Next to me was a table of four: mom, dad, grandma, and teenage son. The son was sitting next to grandma, helping her during dinner. I smiled as I noticed that grandma had a goblet of white wine and a bloody Mary in front of her. There were no cell phones at the table. In fact, I hardly saw a cell phone in the entire restaurant last night—well, except for mine. Their evening started with small portions of fettuccine Alfredo, followed by one sirloin that was sliced by the waiter into small sections and served with roasted potatoes for the table. In the United States, I thought, that steak would be a one-person serving.

Grandma's eyes had that look of certainty about life that we all wish to achieve. Clearly, she was the matriarch. Clearly, the day was so special that the focus was on her at the table. So special that cell phones there and across the restaurant were less important than grandma. Yes, less important than mom too.

I wish I had known to observe the eyes of my mother on occasions such as this. Perhaps I unconsciously did, and that is why I was able to see the eyes of the mothers in Alfredo. Mom is not with me physically any longer, but she is there spiritually every day, and her words of wisdom (and discipline) continue to echo in my head. I toasted her last night as I imagined her sitting across from me, and as I did, my mind moved to the Italian juice glasses and the homemade Italian wine that we would have at times when I was a kid. In hindsight, it was much better than the fourteen-dollar red served in the Riedel stem that I was currently drinking.

Rita

Rita and I go back a long time. I have photos of Rita, her
brother, Gene, and me when my family lived in the yellow
clapboard, brown-shuttered, two-story home on Walnut
Street in Black Lick. Rita was about four years old; I was
about three. It was the first home in which I lived, and its
location was convenient for my dad when he was post-
master in our hometown of Black Lick. That is, we lived
directly behind the post office.

I don't remember a time that I didn't know Rita. I suspect we were in the same playpen together. My cousin
Marla was in that same playpen with us. The connection
that Rita and I share echoes back two or more generations,
before we were even the little ones in that playpen. My
grandparents and Rita's grandparents were friends, probably originating from their roots in the Parma Province
of Italy and eventually settling in the Black Lick-Palmer-
town-Josephine area of Western Pennsylvania.

Our parents were childhood friends. As kids, we would
listen to the stories of their youth, their escapades, their
dating, their swimming at the Coral-Graceton Reservoir,
their marriages. I always recall a story we were told about
Rita's dad singing the song "Goodnight, Irene" to Rita's
mom at the end of an evening with friends. Rita's dad

had a strong, deep voice, and I often wondered what he sounded like when serenading Irene.

The families lived in Palmertown and Josephine, back then thriving subdivisions of Black Lick, towns with lives of their own and community bonds that were strengthened over the years by family intermarriages and the arrival of children. Rita's mom was more like an aunt to me; I can still hear Rita call to my mom, using Mom's nickname, "Hey, Vease."

Between high school graduation and our lives now, Rita and I moved forward in separate directions. Rita was never a distant memory for me; I suspect that I wasn't for her either. Our connection may be spiritual, as we both grew up attending Saint Bonaventure Church in Black Lick, attending catechism classes, riding the catechism bus in the summers for our two-week immersion in our Catholic faith, and watching our families always sit in the same pews. Families did that at St. Bonaventure. If as a kid, you were adventurous, sometimes your parents would permit you to sit with an aunt and uncle in their pew. I always liked to sit with my uncle Pete when I could. Our faith instruction, participation, and community were paramount and not optional.

My connection with Rita could also be from the interrelationship of our family, as my cousins Gloria and Phyllis are also cousins of Rita through their mother, my aunt Dolly (my uncle Pete's beautiful wife). Or maybe our connection is from a horizontal gene transfer that I read about recently, flowing from our grandparents to our parents and to us.

Several weeks ago, I made a quick trip to my childhood hometown of Black Lick to visit with my cousin Marla. An opening occurred in my work and travel schedule, and I jumped on it to see Marla. I spent two wonderful days with Marla, and on my second night, I met my cousin Diana and her husband, Bill, at a restaurant in Indiana, Pennsylvania, for an incredible Italian meal followed by conversation at their home. Diana and I share common family traits, although I was never able to balance her on my extended legs while playing airplane, as she could with me when we were kids.

On my third night, I met Rita at Chestnut Ridge Inn. After not being in touch for too long, we had Facebook to thank for a reconnection several years ago. Addresses were exchanged, and messages began. I like watching Rita post her beautiful cookies and her daughter Tori's photography. Where we would once talk while riding bikes or on swings and slides at the Burrell Elementary School playground, or when playing games with Cousin Marla while sitting cross-legged on the floor of Rita's bedroom, our talks now were of the 2019 kind: texts, emails, and messages on Facebook. With my trip to see Marla scheduled, I emailed Rita to let her know I would be in the area; she wrote back that she would keep her calendar open for me. We agreed on dinner on the patio of the Chestnut Ridge Inn.

When I met Rita at Chestnut Ridge Inn, seeing her standing there for the first time after years, a piece of me came alive again, a piece that had lain dormant for too long. We both stopped and just looked at each other before embracing.

My gosh, it was Rita.

It seemed as if a bolt of energy had rushed through me. Maybe it originated from our grandparents, carried through our parents, and now to us. Maybe our grandparents were looking down and thinking, *Yes, that meaning of family from the old country is still alive.* Not family related by blood, but family related by culture and emotion and sacrifice and hard work and sharing of meals and holidays and open doors and traveling as very young adults to a new country and processing through Ellis Island with little money in your pocket and knowing no one and the name of a town, Black Lick, in a state called Pennsylvania, handwritten on a sheet of paper and held close to your heart. Yes, it seems to me this is the connection that Rita and I share and the foundation on which our friendship was built.

After fifteen minutes of catch-up, our conversation turned to our current lives. Over too many homemade potato chips, dinner, and drinks, we covered a lot in easy conversation as the sun set over forested hills of Western Pennsylvania. When the skies turned dark, a million stars appeared overhead. Yes, the beautiful countryside of Western Pennsylvania. There we were again, years later, still the same core people our parents raised us to be, having the same easy conversation that our parents once shared on their back porches. Punchy and Irene, Bill and Vease must have been looking at each other and smiling.

The night ended with the memory of a New Year's Eve party that my parents threw when we were about nine and ten years old. Our parents and their friends were always known for dressing up and going out for New Year's Eve back then. With Aunt Nellie and Uncle Clarence babysitting us, my brother and I would struggle to stay awake as we waited for Mom and Dad to return, always with horns, noisemakers, hats, and pieces of cake wrapped in paper napkins. This year, Mom and Dad hosted the party at our home, in our 1960s basement turned family room. The kids were not permitted to go down to the family room that night.

Well, Rita and I stood at the top of the stairs, looking down, hearing the music and laughter, looking at each other, and wondering, *Should we?* I knew that if we quietly snuck down the stairs and made a quick right into the laundry room, chances were we would not be caught. We succeeded. Running around the back of the basement to another doorway, we peeked through to see our parents and their friends slow dancing. And kissing! Yes, kissing while dancing!

I remember that we looked at our parents, then looked at each other, somewhat stunned, somewhat bewildered, and somewhat guilty. But grinning. We decided to try to kiss. Afterwards we ran back upstairs to last year's horns, noisemakers, and hats. Midnight was about to strike.

Collections

I am back in Mexico City for two weeks. The air quality is poor. I can feel it in my throat, and now realize the coughing and throat clearing that my colleagues in the office experienced this week wasn't due to an outbreak of colds. I had heard about the poor air quality that affects this beautiful city at times, but this is my first experience with it. I also felt the earth under my feet move a little this past week due to an earthquake off the Pacific coast of Mexico. This is also a periodic occurrence that affects this magnificent city.

As a kid, I collected rocks. Yes, rocks. Any interesting or unconventional rock lying anywhere landed in my pocket, and then in my bedroom, to an appointed location in my rock collection. Obviously, my parents were very tolerant. I also collected leaves in autumn. I walked around Edgemont, my childhood neighborhood, looking for the unusual color of an oak leaf or oversized maple leaf or whatever caught my eye as a young boy whose inherent Gemini traits caused my attention to be diverted to any shiny object or unusual finding. I took the leaves home and showed them to my mom. She helped me press them between layers of waxed paper, after which I admired them for a few weeks, then retired them to my leaf collections from previous years.

I just finished my fifth reading of John Knowles's *A Separate Peace*. It is the book which sparked my interest in reading during my junior year in high school. My parents were avid readers, but the habit of reading for pleasure while acquiring knowledge never developed in me until this book. The story remains with me. On this reading, a paragraph resonated in a different way for me; I decided to save it.

> *"The winter loves me,"* he [Phineas] *retorted, and then, disliking the whimsical sound of that, added, "I mean as much as you can say a season can love. What I mean is, I love winter, and when you really love something, then it loves you back, in whatever way it has to love."*
> (Knowles, 1959, p. 111.)

This paragraph caused me to pause. I looked back on it after finishing the book last night. It says so much. And while I love winter, and while this paragraph justifies in my mind my love of winter, it really transcends the subject stated.

I continue to think about it as I reflect on how this phrase touches life…whether it be a season, a person, a collection of cobalt-blue glass objects that sits in my home, a book, and so on…"it loves [me] back, in whatever way it has to love."

In addition to cobalt-blue glass, I collect books. I appreciate the knowledge, ideas, thoughts, and stories that reside in them. My parents never tossed a book to the garbage, a trait I inherited. If Mom lent one of her books to someone, she expected it to be returned. One time, a book wasn't returned, and she never forgot it or let it rest. I think I also inherited this quality from her. But what was that feeling that Mom had for her books that elicited this strong reaction? "[T]hen it loves you back, in whatever way it has to love."

And I collect quotes. Quotes take up less space, being held in their appointed location in a file on my laptop. And I don't have to press them between layers of waxed paper. They seem to flicker for me as the adult form of a Gemini's shiny objects and unusual findings.

John Knowles's paragraph caused me to look back on a few of my favorite quotes today.

The last two paragraphs of *The Great Gatsby* by F. Scott Fitzgerald:

> *Gatsby believed in the green light, the orgastic future that year by year recedes before us. It eluded us then, but that's no matter — tomorrow we will run faster, stretch out our arms farther... and one fine morning —*

> *So we beat on, boats against the current, borne back ceaselessly into the past.* (Fitzgerald, 1925, p. 180.)

The last line of Ayn Rand's *The Fountainhead*:

> *Then there was only the ocean and the sky and the figure of Howard Roark.* (Rand, 1943, p. 754.)

I've read *Gatsby* several times. I am now on my sixth reading of *The Fountainhead*. It is a book that has served as a source of inspiration for me over my life, after being awestruck by it on my first reading during my morning subway commutes to Macy's, my first employer in Manhattan. I didn't want the subway ride to end before I finished a chapter, despite the very poor conditions and lack of air-conditioning in the subways back then. Yes, sometimes I could perspire through my suit jacket on my morning treks to work, but my book took my mind away from my environment and into another land, another place, another series of sentences, some of which I would record among my collection of quotes for future reference.

And so the John Knowles quote from *A Separate Peace* has now entered my quote collection.

What is it that causes some phrases to resonate deeply within our psyche and remain there, surfacing at times, then submerging themselves back into our subconsciousness? What is it that causes the stories in some books to stick, forcing us to take a book off the shelf and read it again...and again?

Perhaps it is the grounding they provide or the thoughts or inspirations they provoke. Or, perhaps, "then it loves you back, in whatever way it has to love."

Adulthood

I am in Mexico City again this week. On Thursday, we had an earthquake drill at the office. At 10:00 a.m., a jolting alarm sounded. We all moved to an interior wall and were asked by a guard to count off; I was *numero trece*. Thanks to my seatmate, she announced my number to the guard as I stumbled once again with my Spanish. We then turned and in a very orderly and respectful manner, began descending an endless flight of stairs, finally exiting the building in a line. Even in a drill such as this, the Mexican people exhibited a level of politeness by which I am constantly amazed.

My floormates formed a group next to another guard who held a sign indicating Piso 4; we were four deep, about thirty across, as were all other floor groups, and about 300 yards from the office building. Each floor group was separated by three employees dressed in blue tunics. I remembered the notice that I received in my hotel room, the night prior, from the general manager announcing a drill at ten the next day. I read it and dismissed it, as I knew I would not be in the hotel at that time. I now understand that drill was a citywide earthquake drill.

As I stood there, I looked up at the building and wondered, *What if?* I thought about the last earthquake in

Mexico City in 2017, in which buildings crumbled around some of the same people beside whom I stood. I wondered how the people felt on the Brooklyn Bridge on September 11, 2001, as they turned to see one of the towers fall. I saw people around me that day—lives I knew existed, but about which I knew nothing—all doing what I was doing, just not necessarily speaking English as their first language. I remembered a few instances during my time in Mexico City when the earth did move a slight bit under my feet, and once when an alarm went off, signaling a possible earthquake. Sometimes, your awareness as an adult is too real.

One Saturday morning when I was in my twenties and visiting my parents, I remember my mom sitting at the kitchen table, having her coffee as she always did. Mom always used a coffee cup. A little milk. One teaspoon of sugar. She opened the mail from the day before and read it while enjoying her wake-up coffee. Dad drank his coffee from a green- and white-striped mug, always sitting in his easy chair while watching the early morning news. I had my black coffee in another green-and-white mug and took my assigned seat, since childhood, at the kitchen table.

Dad entered to refill his coffee. Mom looked up, and for some reason, that morning I said, "You know, you never told me how hard being an adult was."

Mom looked at me with eyes that registered, *"You've got to be kidding,"* seemingly signaling the knowledge that her oldest son was now aware of the meaning of adulthood.

I often wondered later in life why the conversations of my parents with their siblings and friends always returned to the health of their contemporaries. Years ago, while visiting two college friends one weekend at their home, I mentioned to the mother of one of them that all my parents seemed to focus on was the health of their family and friends.

Mrs. Lewis looked at me and said, "Someday, you will understand."

I now do.

There is something different about reaching a certain age and suddenly finding yourself and your cousins and friends confronted with health issues, versus living through the health-related matters of your parents and their generation. These are people you studied beside in high school and college, partied too hard with, shared hangovers with, and ate greasy foods with at Denny's those mornings to counter the hangovers, took too many chances with, laughed and danced with at their weddings, were excited with the birth of their children, attended the weddings of their kids, and have a myriad of other shared experiences about which to reminisce. Conversations and experiences over life evolved, but the threads of friendship remained, and conversations, although months and sometimes years apart, seemed as if you were picking up from where you left off yesterday. In looks, we never aged to each other.

My mom's friend Irene passed at an early age. I remember my parents taking me to the hospital to see her once. I was not permitted into her room; instead, I sat in the hallway outside of it while Mom and Dad visited. I felt the intensity of my parents' feelings when they departed that room. It was a new feeling for me. When Irene passed, her daughter Rita was my first friend to lose a parent; I remember my mom speaking with concern and caring about Irene to her sisters during Irene's illness. When she passed, Mom took it hard. I felt her loss, but perhaps was too young to understand that this was someone she may have studied beside in high school, maybe partied too hard with, once shared a hangover or two with, took chances with, laughed and danced with at her wedding, was excited at the birth of her children, and so on.

Mom and Dad kept extensive baby books for my brother and me; nestled in mine is a card from Irene and her husband, Punchy, congratulating them on my birth. I was outside of Irene's hospital room that evening because I was the embodiment and extension of another connection that Mom and Irene shared. I had to be there. Mom and Dad wanted me there.

I think that, later in life, adulthood forces the resurfacing of deep-rooted connections that we formed early in life with our friends and cousins, but of which we are mostly unaware until, one day, the health of one of them, or two of them, or your own health becomes the subject of all too frequent conversations. Your journey in life together enters a new phase.

You care, but it is a caring that has had years to germinate. You are concerned, but it is visceral concern. You pray. You find yourself jumping from the health of one friend to the health of a cousin, to the health of another friend over dinner, over breakfast, after a movie. Their well-being becomes your well-being. Their fears become your fears. Their milestones are your milestones. There is no "let's go to Denny's for eggs and bacon" to cure a hangover any longer. But I wish there were.

Friends and family now often hear me say, "We are our parents' age." Perhaps it is that age when we realize that your awareness as an adult is too real. You also realize that you would not want it any other way.

Jet Engines

At five eighteen this morning, the sounds of jet engines were outside my forty-second-floor window in New York City. I had already been awake since four twenty-five, when a dream sounded an alarm bell that stirred me from my sleep, from which I never recovered. My initial thought when hearing the jet engine sound was that New York City was under attack. Unlike Papa in Clemente Clarke Moore's "A Visit from St. Nicholas" (a.k.a. "'Twas the Night before Christmas"), I jumped up, panicked, and peered out the window, scoping the dark sky for planes. None were to be seen. With my window facing the Queens Midtown Tunnel, I looked down to see if the tunnel was flooding; the noise might have been from pumps extracting water, similar to the time after Hurricane Sandy. Nothing.

Finally, at Thirty-Sixth Street and First Avenue, I saw steam billowing out of the pavement. A steam pipe must have exploded. Fire trucks and police cars were surrounding the area. Traffic was being diverted. The jet-engine sound lasted two hours. It was the steam escaping from the pipes.

As I sat having my coffee and looking over another day of jolting news reports in the *New York Times*, I realized I was tired. Tired not from the loss of sleep, which tends to elude me at this age, but tired from the emotions of the morning's immediate reaction to the sounds of what I perceived to be a plane.

For those of us aware of and around on September 11, 2001, I think planes are a trigger. I doubt if anyone who experienced that event can look up and see a plane flying over Manhattan on a clear, blue-sky day and not have a pinprick of panic. Certainly, the perception of the sounds of a plane outside your window can have another deeper effect.

As a kid, I sometimes peered into the Western Pennsylvania skies while playing outside, and occasionally I saw a plane fly overhead, backdropped by a clear-blue sky and white, fluffy clouds. For me, then, the idea of a plane and the experience of flying in one was a dream, something beyond my grasp, a mystery and a marvel that one day I hoped to experience.

I finally did experience the thrill of flying. But that day in September 2001 took the childhood thoughts about planes from me and turned them into something about which to be concerned. Something now to be feared at times. Perhaps Mom and Dad felt the same after December 7, 1941.

I watched the 1964 Peter Sellers movie *Dr. Strangelove* a few years ago. I now consider it required viewing. The world has changed and continues to feel unsteady on so many levels. The movie left an impression on me. This morning, my initial reaction was not surprise when I perceived the sound of a jet engine outside of my window. I realize now that my initial feeling was, *It's happening.*

Vitamin D and Volcanoes

I am in Mexico City again. October 15 came and went. This is the day I start taking vitamin D supplements for the winter, given that the fluorescent lighting of office environments does not provide the same benefits as the sun.

My cousin Linda Marshall Bonya suggested these supplements to me when she and I both found ourselves with low vitamin D readings several years ago post our annual physicals. Linda passed away in 2017 after a noble and hard-fought twelve-year battle with breast cancer. With October being Breast Cancer Awareness Month, I am fortunate to have this annual event of our shared vitamin ritual to once again remember her. As I stated in her eulogy, "We were cousins by birth, best friends by choice."

As I write this in front of my window on the thirty-ninth floor of the hotel, I am staring at the volcano Popocatépetl in the distance. This morning it was emitting smoke and steam again. I was told not to worry about the emissions when I first saw them, as they are the result of the volcano releasing energy. This is a good thing. Popocatépetl last erupted in March of this year; I watched smoke and ash billow out of her as I sat having breakfast at this same hotel.

As a boy from Black Lick, Pennsylvania, you would think that my reaction would have been stronger to the activity of Popocatépetl. Early in life, the most serious Mother Nature event for me was lightning, a bolt of which I once witnessed come through an open window of our 1960s basement family room of my childhood home; it aimed directly at our blonde-wood, black-and-white television.

My uncle Pete Bernini passed away in 1977, at the young age of sixty-eight. I remember the look on my aunt Dolly's face as we departed their home, where the family had gathered that afternoon after the funeral. He was my mom's first sibling to move on to the next life, and the uncle that I liked to sit beside at times in church.

As Dad drove over the bridge connecting the town of Josephine, where Uncle Pete and Aunt Dolly lived, and the town of Black Lick, where we lived, my mom, dad, brother, and I looked to the left to see a wall of water coming at the car. In Johnstown, Pennsylvania, a dam was again breached due to heavy rains. The water came crashing twenty-three miles downstream into Black Lick. To drive forward would be to drive into deeper water. To back up wasn't an option, as my dad later said that he quickly thought the engine might stall and the rising water prevent us from opening the doors.

Dad calmly said to Mom, "Grab everything out of the glove compartment."

As water rose around us, we waded to a dry area on the Josephine side of the bridge. I ran to Aunt Dolly's home for help, while my parents and brother watched the once gentle, serene waters of the Black Lick Creek submerge our 1976 red Mercury Montego with a white-vinyl opera roof. My cousins still remember the paleness of my face when I arrived breathless at Aunt Dolly's home.

The lightning bolt that struck our black-and-white television was truly an act of nature. The breached dam was a shared act of human decision and nature; I say this as Johnstown has a history of devastating floods, the worst of which was again recorded recently in a book by Al Roker.

After my apartment building in Manhattan was evacuated on the eve of Hurricane Sandy, I started to seriously wonder how many of these types of events were caused by human decisions to which nature subsequently responded. Many of us remember the Parkay margarine commercial in which a lovely woman in a serene woodland setting, birds chirping around her, stated, "It's not nice to fool Mother Nature." There seems to be some truth in her words.

The East River rose and flooded up to Second Avenue in the city, immersing the lobby of my apartment building and much of the Lower East Side in four feet or more of water. Most of Lower Manhattan south of Forty-Second Street, including the New York University Hospital complex, was without electricity for weeks. I remember what seemed to be hundreds of ambulances lined up to move patients from the hospital after Sandy moved out to sea, leaving behind nature's beautiful, calm, clear-blue skies. I hear Maureen McGovern's voice in the background now, singing "There's Got to be a Morning After," as I type this;

although, in reality, music was far from my thoughts that morning.

A few months ago, I started to read a history of Mexico City, but had to stop. The Aztecs had their unique culture, as we all do, and as I read their rituals, my reactions were visceral. I am sure they had their methods to appease Popocatépetl to prevent her from erupting, but I stopped short of reading about them as I realized that I really didn't need to know what they were. Culturally, the Aztecs were hardly primitive; they understood that prevention, however they attempted to do it, was better than dealing with the aftermath. There is something here for our advanced culture to learn.

I am constantly amazed how monies are found to rebuild a collapsed bridge, but none to be found to rebuild it before a collapse occurs. I am amazed at the amount of profits made by health insurance companies, when some or more of those profits could be spent on preventive research to mitigate the later payouts for hospitalizations and medications. I am amazed that new prisons can be funded, but teachers must buy their own school supplies, when better educational systems are known to prevent crime. I am amazed at the cost of a college education, when I have witnessed kids with degrees who cannot spell or use a calculator, only to first fail themselves, then fail their employer, then find themselves collecting unemployment. And I am amazed at how much money is put into the creation of online and phone surveys, when the monies would be better spent on comprehensive professional training of customer service associates.

Something seems to be out of whack.

Perhaps we have moved too far from one of the meanings of the term "insurance." Definition number two in the online Merriam-Webster dictionary (Remember that big, dusty book with the musty-smelling pages in your high school library?) is "a means of guaranteeing protection or safety."

I think Merriam-Webster should move definition number two to the number-one position. I think, too, that it needs to be followed by Ben Franklin's famous saying: "An ounce of prevention is worth a pound of cure." And that is why Linda and I have taken vitamin D during the winter for years.

Doug

A wise man once told me that he read that there are three types of people you meet in life: The Right Person for the Right Moment, The Right Person for the Right Time, The Right Person Forever.

Doug passed away recently. He is the brother of my childhood friend Nancy. Doug may not have remembered me, but through his influence, he left a mark on me that has lasted my lifetime.

When Nancy and I were in fourth grade at Burrell Elementary School, it was time for us to select an instrument to learn to play. The music instructor was patient with his lot of well-behaved kids. I remember that those of us who wanted to learn to play an instrument paraded single file onto the stage at the school, and each told our would-be instructor their decision. One of my best friends, Joey, was ahead of me and chose the trumpet. I was clueless as I stood there, sweating about which instrument to declare, but firmly knowing I wanted to learn to play an instrument.

Nancy was directly in front of me and stated her desire for the saxophone, as her brother played it. Sounded good to me, and so I played the saxophone all the way through my senior year. I remember my dad's reaction that night when I told him my musical instrument selection over dinner. He simply said, "Couldn't you have picked a less expensive instrument?"

Later that fourth-grade year, Nancy told me about the hamster litter that she and Doug had and offered one of the babies to me. Mom and Dad agreed, and after a trip to Woolworths to buy a cage, food, etc., we went to Nancy and Doug's home for the adoption. In addition to meeting my new hamster, I met Doug for the first time. On the kitchen table sat a new jar of Jif peanut butter, the plastic cap of which held a mesmerizing array of gift-with-purchase marbles. We weren't a peanut butter family, but I needed to have the Jif peanut butter with the gift-with-purchase marbles. So the Olson household acquired a jar for me. The peanut butter sat well on a Ritz. I never did learn to play marbles.

Recalling the characters from Charles Schultz's *Peanuts* comic strip, if I were Charlie Brown, Nancy was my Peggy Jean, the little redheaded love interest of Charlie, except that Nancy was blonde. We spent a lot of time together in grade school. Nancy's mother saved poetry that we wrote together in third grade. Nancy sent copies to me many years ago when we got reacquainted; when I showed the poems to my mom, she smiled wide with that remembrance smile that mothers have. I am not sure that I was really "in love" with Nancy, but I was enamored with her creativity, her artistic abilities, her intelligence, and her approach to life back then. What I remember most about those days, though, was her smile.

I met Doug again when we entered our freshman year in high school. Doug was a senior. Doug held the coveted first-saxophone, first-seat position in the saxophone section of the band, with a very pretty upperclassman by the name of Bobbie in the second seat. I was all the way back in the second seat of the second-saxophone section, behind my saxophone archrival, Janice. Yep, all the way down the row.

I remember watching Doug play the saxophone. It was an extension of him; he moved smoothly with the sounds it emitted and mastered that hand-eye coordination between the notes on his music sheets, the baton of the band conductor, and as lead sax, the rest of his saxophone section. His fingers glided smoothly over the keys while his body moved with the music.

Being of smaller stature, I had to reach with my pinky finger to make some of the lower notes on my saxophone. I knew I wanted to have Doug's talents, but I also knew that as an awkward teenager, it would be a challenge for me to gain his sense of rhythm and command over the music. My first goal: move up one chair and move Janice back one chair. Janice and I shared a love-hate relationship in the band room for the next four years.

During freshman year, Bobbie encouraged me to try out for the pit band to support the school's annual musical production, which that year was *Calamity Jane*. I did, and I won the first saxophone, second seat, next to Bobbie's first seat. I learned a lot from her during that time.

Doug was dating a young lady named Colleen, Calamity herself, the star of the show. Doug was taller than I, had a smooth gait and a very easy attitude about life. I hoped that one day I could also achieve that style and composure…and maybe date the star of the high school musical. It didn't happen. I did, however, later in my high school career, go on to play lead sax in the jazz band, which was almost equally rewarding for me.

Tall, smooth movements and an easy attitude were not in my genes. But among those genes was a love of saxophone music, and this is thanks to Doug's influence on his little sister, Nancy, and Nancy's influence on me that fateful day in fourth grade on the Burrell Elementary stage.

I learned later that my uncle Mario played saxophone in local swing bands during the 1940s before he was drafted into the service and went to war. His wife, my mom's sister Della, once told me that when she met Uncle Mario while he was playing at a local dance hall, she decided right then that she was marrying that handsome saxophone player.

I also learned later that my cousin Donna Jean played saxophone while in high school. Sometime during my junior-high years, I acquired her orange-and-black high-school band jacket with an embroidered saxophone on it. It was kismet. The planets aligned for my destiny with the saxophone.

I love the smooth sounds of a sax. For me, it simply sings. By far, John Klemmer is my favorite saxophone artist, but over the years, I have come to love Glenn

Miller's orchestra, Billy Vaughn, and Kenny G almost equal to John Klemmer. Even as harmony, the sounds of a saxophone can stop me in my tracks, forcing me to take a moment to breathe and listen.

So, Doug, this is the legacy you left behind within me. In return, I offer you John Klemmer's "Touch," a fitting tribute for how your life once touched that fourth-grader as the Right Person for the Right Moment.

Neighbors

As of this month, I have consulted with my Mexico City client for two years. The time has flown. Today is a Monday holiday in Mexico, and I am working from my hotel room. The country is celebrating Revolution Day, which commemorates a ten-year revolution, which began in 1910 to end the struggle against the thirty-five-year reign of dictator José de la Cruz Porfirio Diaz Mori. The uprising began when Diaz jailed his presidential opponent, Francisco Madero, a wealthy landowner. Madero then initiated the uprising. The holiday is celebrated on the third Monday of November, near the official date of November 20.

Working here, I have come to understand that my Mexican coworkers know almost every holiday celebrated in the United States. And, they pretty much know why we celebrate the holidays, even Thanksgiving, which may be our most unique holiday. I can't say that I know the same about Mexican holidays and, much to my surprise, Cinco de Mayo is not a recognized holiday here.

When thinking more about this, I also realized that while working in Toronto for a number of years, my Canadian coworkers also knew about the holidays in the

United States. I, again, didn't know about their holidays, except for Victoria Day.

Once when Kim, my business partner, and I were having a conversation with our Canadian coworkers, I made a comment in which I referred to myself as an American. One of our coworkers quickly corrected me by stating that she was an American too. She went on to say that the population of the entire Western Hemisphere are Americans. She was right. It was presumptuous of me and of anyone to usurp the title of American because we are from the United States.

I never forgot this, and now consciously refer to myself as from the United States. I thought later that we often refer to Europeans, which is all-encompassing for the European community. Why not refer to all of us from the Western Hemisphere as Americans? That is what we are.

Which leads me to once again consider that our education systems in the United States do not require second languages to be learned. With Quebec to our north speaking French, and almost every country to our south speaking Spanish, it seems to me that these languages are becoming more and more necessary to know as the world contracts, and especially as it contracts on our side of the globe. All I need to do is look out of my hotel window across the business district here in Mexico City to see a sea of company logos from the United States and Europe on the exterior of office buildings.

Realizing that our Canadian and Mexican neighbors know about the United States holidays, but we know little about theirs, I also think now that perhaps our education systems do not spend enough time teaching the history and cultures of our closest neighbors. Maybe if all three countries could create a combined educational course on the history of North America and make it a requirement in secondary education in each of the three countries, together with a second-language requirement, all three countries could benefit from these common historical and communication bridges. We share much, and there is much to be learned. Maybe by mandating these requirements for children today, our future as North Americans could become the force the world needs.

I really do wonder if the United States, Mexico, and Canada could ever combine talents and emerge at the forefront of the world stage in technology, education, agriculture, health care, cybersecurity, infrastructure, and climate. With the talents among the three countries, we could, in my opinion, become a true force of leading change in the world for the betterment of global society. We would first need to learn to appreciate the skills, knowledge, and talents of each other, then break down the artificial barriers that separate us as countries, while maintaining our defining borders.

Note that I purposely omitted trade from my list. I think this is where hang-ups begin. Perhaps if we were more seamless in our approach to trade, and were to build it on a foundation that requires all three countries to equally and concurrently benefit, many bumps along the way would be smoothed. We tend to get hung up on who gets the better deal when talking trade among our three countries.

But before all this, we need fearless, selfless, visionary leaders in lockstep with each other for all three countries to drive this initiative.

After all, we are all the same people, with the same goals—trying to make a decent living in roles that positively challenge us, provide for our families, and put a little money away for the future. We in North America all get up in the mornings on this side of the world to the same sun rising and go to sleep at night to the same sun setting. There is no difference in the majority of us.

But as I return home through JFK Airport from Mexico each month, I am routed through one of three lanes for Customs: Global Entry, United States and Canadian Citizens, and All Others. I question each time I pass through Customs why our Mexican neighbors are not included in the line designated as United States and Canadian Citizens. Why is this? I have no explanation. I feel embarrassment when it is mentioned to me by my Mexican coworkers.

Just some thoughts on my second anniversary here in Mexico City. Here is a nod to my neighbors in Mexico and a nod to my neighbors in Canada.

¡Tenga un buen día! Passe une bonne journée!

Cats

I am back in Mexico City.

I recently saw the movie *Cats*. I am not sure why the critics didn't like it, but I often disagree with what they say about movies. I am also not sure why it didn't receive stronger attendance. I liked it, and although it didn't hold completely true to the original Broadway show, it was good in its own right and close enough for me.

The theater was full, and I noticed most of the audience was older. I find this to be the case with good movies in which things aren't blowing up; they tend to attract older audiences and fill the theaters. Funny, Hollywood hasn't figured out that formula. After all, the older generations were raised on movies in theaters. It is what you did on a date.

There were three young women sitting in front of me. They laughed loud and hard throughout most of the movie. I found it annoying, especially when they laughed at the more serious moments. When Judi Dench's character, Grizabella, first appeared, I thought they would bust a gut. I guess they thought the movie was a comedy. It isn't. At one of the more serious moments, when laughter came from the three, someone in the theater started clapping their hands in an effort to stop them from their riotous laughter. I sat there wondering if they were aware they were the only three people in a full theater who were laughing.

Cats holds a special place in my heart. It was the first Broadway show I saw when I first moved to New York City. I saw it on New Year's Eve, which, again, was my first in New York City. Betty Buckley was in the starring role, and I was amazed that the mother from the 1970s TV show *Eight is Enough* was there on stage in front of me. And then, if that wasn't enough, through the magic of Broadway, she ascended from the stage, up and over the audience, and into the ceiling of the theater as her character was lifted up to the Heaviside Layer. I was mesmerized, only to have the magic of the evening continue when I departed the Winter Garden Theater into the throngs of people gathered for the ball dropping in Times Square. For a boy from Black Lick, Pennsylvania, now in the big city, the memories of that evening are still special to me. It was a beginning.

I saw *Cats* on Broadway three times. The last time was when my cousin Linda brought her son Neal to New York to celebrate his thirteenth birthday. We went to see *Cats* and were fortunate to get front-row seats right on the aisle. During the show, the starring white cat came down from the stage, and as part of her performance, slinked around Neal as a cat would do. For a thirteen-year-old boy, this was a life-defining moment. I can still see the big, broad smile on Neal's face as the white cat curled up to him.

I am sure the story circulated quickly and widely around his high school on his return home.

During that same birthday celebration, we took Neal to Windows on the World, the restaurant at the top of the former World Trade Center. We had a window seat facing north into the city. It was an awesome view of New York. Before we left for the restaurant, I reminded Neal of the gentlemanly things to do that evening: hold the chair for his mother when she sat, stand if she stood to leave the table and stand when she returned until she was again seated, and tip the attendant in the men's room a dollar when he handed him a towel to dry his hands. This last one was a challenge for Neal, as I remember him saying, "A whole dollar?!"

The most touching part of the evening, though, was when Neal handed the coat-check attendant another dollar, retrieved Linda's coat, and held it for her as she put it on. She looked at him with tears in her eyes and said, "My little boy is growing up." The moment is still emotional for me.

Jennifer Hudson did an amazing performance of the song "Memory" in the movie *Cats*. Her enunciation was clear, and for the first time, I heard all the words. It is a powerful song, but hearing all the words for the first time made me realize just how powerful it truly is. Her rendition took me back to hearing Betty Buckley sing it on Broadway. Fortunately for the audience in the theater that day, the three young women remained silent during Ms. Hudson's performance. After the movie, I returned home and researched the lyrics. I wonder if Andrew Lloyd

Webber and Trevor Nunn realized when they set T.S. Eliot's poem to music, the power, universal relevance, and soul-touching lyrics of what they had just completed?

This past year, I returned to Western Pennsylvania to visit family, including my aunt Helen, my cousins Sarah Kay and Diana, and my childhood friend Rita. While there, I stopped by Beacon Ridge, an assisted-living facility in Indiana, Pennsylvania, to share lunch with some of the residents. It was a moving and rewarding experience as I listened intensely to the stories of some of the residents as we ate. One gentleman was excited to learn I was from New York City and told me of his numerous trips there for his career as a young man. Another lovely woman, who knew my aunt Nellie, told me of her life in Homer City. As we enjoyed our chicken, yams, green beans, and a very measured slice of bread pudding (I declined the vanilla sauce), I noticed the sparkle in the eyes of those who were speaking to me. They all had smiles on their faces as they reminisced. Some sat just staring at me, with eyes that registered, but voices that couldn't speak in the same way any longer. All they seemed to want to do was to talk to me. Just someone to talk to.

And as I got up to leave the table, one lovely woman reached across with her ninety-four-year-old hand and placed it on mine…a hand that may have once held a jump rope and dolls, a hand that held a bouquet of flowers on her wedding day and felt the first life of her newborn children, a hand that washed too many dishes and too many clothes while finding time to feel soil as it planted flowers and vegetables, a hand that hung ornaments on

Christmas trees and placed graduation mortarboards on her children's heads, a hand that passed her children to their new spouses, a hand that was once steady as it lifted a fine porcelain tea cup, a hand that embraced the hand of a husband during his last moments of life. She had a sparkle in her eyes, but no words. She just reached over to touch my hand. And as I read the lyrics to "Memory" after seeing the movie *Cats*, I thought of her.

Thank you, Andrew Lloyd Webber.

Memories Not Spoken

I recently watched a PBS rebroadcast of a concert by the group America, which was filmed at the London Palladium. It brought back memories of sitting in my college dorm room in Aurelius Hall, freshman year, studying at my desk. My room consisted of bunk beds, a sink and mirror, and a closet that was too small for two roommates. Aurelius was an old hall; it survived the devastating Saint Vincent College fire of 1963. The woodwork was real, and our door had a working transom above it, indicating the age of the building and providing airflow on those hot nights before air-conditioning was installed. My roommate and I shared a small window that opened outward to a view of the field on which the Pittsburgh Steelers trained in the summer.

My desk was next to the door. Above my desk, I had a built-in shelf that housed my books. The desk was illuminated by a gooseneck lamp that sat to my right. I had a Westinghouse digital clock radio centered on my desk, from which emanated the songs of the day when I wasn't focused on my studies.

I loved anything from America that year (and still do). And I remember how I detested "Muskrat Love" by Captain and Tennille and "I Shot the Sheriff" by Eric

Clapton, being forced to turn down the volume on my
clock radio when those songs began to air. My uncle Allie
bought the clock radio from the company store that once
was in the Westinghouse plant outside of Blairsville, Pennsylvania. Uncle Allie worked most of his career in that
plant. He bought the clock radio at the request of my mom
and dad, for them to give to me as a gift when I entered
my freshman year of college. I remember how excited
I was with this new technology. It was digital!

As I watched America on PBS, I thought of a paper
I researched and composed for my twentieth-century history class while sitting at that desk during my freshman
year of college. In high school, history classes never pro-
gressed beyond the Reconstruction for some reason. Perhaps there was never enough time in the school year to
go beyond Reconstruction. My first real understanding
of both World Wars came from Mr. Manoli's freshman
history class at eight in the morning, three days a week,
when I started college. Fortunately, his classroom was in a
building adjacent and connected to Aurelius Hall, so my
roommate and I could just roll out of bed at 7:45 a.m. and
make it to class on time. This was all before bedhead was
a look that young men strove to achieve.

My paper was on the Night of Long Knives. I bought
a book, the author of which I no longer remember, which
served as the foundation of my research. This paper was
the first time I studied World War II in any real way, with
any depth. I remember my gut-wrenching feelings as
I read of the devastation of the Jewish communities as the
Nazis destroyed everything in their path for a reason that

was beyond my known comprehension. What remained when the Nazis were done were shattered homes and businesses and lives. Unthinkable acts. What repeated in my consciousness after completing the book was the shattering—no, utter destruction—of any sense of security that the Jewish population in Germany could hold in their hearts and minds. Unsafe. Period. That moment of realization is still with me.

My dad was in World War II. So was my uncle Mario, who served on the *Bon Homme Richard* battleship in the Pacific. My uncle Reno was in North Africa and later moved up through Italy, marching forward for the liberation of my grandparents' homeland. My uncle Dutch also served in Italy. They all saw action. Dad was in the medical corps moving through France.

Neither my dad nor any of my uncles ever spoke about their time in World War II. Never. Not a word was spoken during their back-porch or kitchen-table conversations, nor while walking around their gardens together, perusing the growth of their tomato plants, nor while working together to reshingle a roof or build a garage. Not a recollection was mentioned about World War II when going through my parents' photo albums with them in our living room, all of us viewing photos of my dad in his army uniform, with his buddies while he was stationed in France.

I never thought to ask about Dad's time in the army during World War II, and in hindsight, as a curious kid, that surprises me. Perhaps my lack of questioning was because we never got to World War II in my middle school or high school history classes. But then, maybe it was due to the decisions of my dad and my uncles to never discuss it around my cousins or me, therefore never sparking a curiosity in us to ask questions.

I imagine the sights and sounds were just too much to bear thinking about and reliving after the realities of the war were behind my dad and my uncles. Maybe they wanted to spare their kids from hearing about the atrocities and horrors of this war, the war they lived through day after day after day while shielding their ears from the screeching of bombs and the roar of enemy plane engines overhead, when realizing that "duck and cover" was suddenly an innate full-body, ongoing reaction, while witnessing devastation of both buildings and human bodies, while passing displaced souls seeking food and shelter and loved ones missing among the ruins, when burying friends and strangers alike while soldiering on each day without enough sleep or rest or food, but with too much, perhaps way too much, unrelenting fear? Maybe, too, they wanted to protect us for as long as possible from knowledge of what came to be known as the Holocaust, the ultimate horror coming after the Night of Long Knives.

From my studies, readings, and multiple documentaries to which I am addicted, I now understand what happened in World War II. And I learned of it from my friend Andrea when she and her husband made a trip to Auschwitz and saw her husband's family name on luggage there.

Years have passed since I sat in Aurelius Hall writing that paper and listening to America on my Westinghouse clock radio. I always liked studying and remember grieving that time somewhat as my college days came to a close. I give my parents the credit of instilling in me a quest for knowledge, but with that came a quest for understanding. Something switched within me during that time at my desk while writing my paper on the Night of Long Knives. It wasn't so much reporting events any longer to achieve a grade, but a visceral drive to know why, one that transcends the quest for a grade. For that moment, I am grateful.

Suits

I miss wearing suits. When I started my career many years ago, suits were the required dress for men. Getting ready in the mornings was so easy. I always knew which ties went with which shirts to wear with which suits. Not a lot of thought had to take place after my morning shower. I realize as I write this that women didn't have it so easy then.

I was alarmed when casual dress was first introduced. For those of us guys who lived through this trauma, suddenly decisions had to be made as to which shirt to wear with the khakis today. *How do I make this look different? Add a sweater? Which one? Maybe a navy blazer? Maybe I should just put a suit on and forget about it?*

Since those days, I have adjusted, of course. I still miss wearing a suit. Most of my clients have casual dress codes, but that, for me, is now grey or navy, lightweight wool trousers and a long-sleeve, button-down shirt. I tend to wear a blazer, but it doesn't remain on me most days.

I was very impressed with the dress at my client's office in Mexico City. The staff dressed...really dressed...in many instances as if it were the 1980s again when power dressing was in vogue. Everyone always looked polished and put together. Even for casual office dress, guys took a nice pair of dark-washed jeans, paired them with a crisp button-front shirt and a great sports jacket, and made this look over-the-top great by adding a distinctive designer belt or designer loafers.

My friend Maria consulted with this same client and once told me that she was always amazed how guys in our client's office could put on a great pair of jeans and a fashion tee, and by just throwing a great looking scarf around their necks, look incredible. In the United States, guys tend not to wear a great scarf with a tee and jeans. The look, though, is lost without it.

When I started my career, I had two and one-half suits. The half suit was a charcoal-grey wool-flannel that I purchased in graduate school for interviews. I didn't realize at the time that it wouldn't translate to summer. I bought it at Saks Fifth Avenue in Downtown Pittsburgh, where I was going to school. I paid three hundred dollars for it. It was way too much for an unemployed, no-job-prospects student who was up to his neck in student loans. I decided not to mention the price to my mom and dad. Saks actually gave me the credit to buy it. Maybe they had pity on a poor graduate student. Maybe the credit department wasn't looking that day at my credit eligibility. I paid it off in small increments. I thought I looked phenomenal in it; so did the sales associate who sold it to me. Yellow ties at that time were *de rigueur* as power ties. I bought a yellow foulard at the same time to complement my way-too-expensive suit. I was ready. Bring on the interviews!

One of my other two suits was a charcoal-grey, double-breasted pinstripe. It was a year-round suit. I have no recollection as to when or where or why I bought it. I always felt as if something weren't right with it. As most know, when wearing anything double breasted, you are forced to keep it buttoned. When unbuttoned, the excess material of the jacket front is always in the way, always flopping around, always making me feel as if the suit were too large. I wasn't comfortable sitting with the jacket buttoned, so often I found myself forgetting to button it after sitting through a meeting. Walking down a hallway, I would realize the front of my jacket was flapping in the air.

It wasn't until later that I understood what wasn't right about that suit. Working in the fashion industry, I learned that if you are five foot eight inches tall or under, double-breasted suit jackets will give the illusion that you are shorter than you are. The jacket was cutting off my height. I mistakenly, in a moment of weakness, only bought one other double-breasted suit. I had the same feeling that it wasn't right, but this time I spent the money on it when I should have known better.

My third suit I bought in Philadelphia for grad school. It was medium blue, single-breasted. I didn't know that I should have bought a navy-blue pinstripe or charcoal-grey pinstripe for an MBA program. I may have been the only guy in a medium-blue suit in our class photo book. Such is life. This suit was a favorite of mine, and when I started my first job, I wore it a lot. Well, I alternated nine months of the year with the double-breasted and this suit. For three months in winter, I also had the flannel.

One night after work and at a popular nightspot in Manhattan (straight from work, briefcase in tow), I backed into someone's lit cigarette. My favorite suit now had a burn hole in the back of the jacket. I couldn't afford to replace it. *C'est la vie.* A few people in the office commented on my burn hole, but most were respectful not to mention it.

Power ties evolved into designer ties my first year at work, and I saved a little to buy one. I scoured the selling floor of Macy's Herald Square store for a tie that would perfectly complement my burn-hole suit. I finally found a designer tie at a price that was "reasonably within reason"; at least, that's what I convinced myself. At thirty-five dollars, it was a perfect match to my burn-hole suit and to my tastes. I am sure in today's prices it would be $235. After paying for it, the sales associate professionally wrapped it in tissue paper and gingerly placed it in a Macy's aubergine-colored bag for my transport home. I couldn't wait to wear it the next day.

That next day, I pressed the white shirt I planned to wear with my new tie, then showered and dressed. I felt great and looked great, my new tie taking focus away from the burn hole in my suit. Sharp. Put together. I had a meeting with the vice president of my division that day. He had a reputation for cutting off the ties of the guys who worked for him if he didn't like their ties. I never witnessed this happening, but had heard enough about it to be wary of my tie selections each day. But that day, I knew I was safe in my new designer tie.

When I walked into his office for the meeting, his first sentence to me was, "Where'd you get that tie?" I knew where this was heading with my brand-new designer tie, for which I paid way too much on my salary to have it cut off.

* * *

As a freshman in high school, as the spring months rolled into late May and early June, my mom added to my wardrobe to better manage classes in a high school that lacked air-conditioning. One new shirt was a particular favorite of mine, and I was eager to wear it. I have wavy hair, and back then I wore it longer, over my ears. For anyone born with wavy hair, you will understand when I say that there are days you win control of your hair, and days your hair ignores your pleas and does what it wants to do. On the day of the introductory wearing of the new shirt that Mom bought for me, my hair was obeying me. I felt good, and I thought I looked good. Sharp. Put together. All was right in the world of my freshman appearance.

While sitting in the auditorium, waiting for one of those high school auditorium events to begin, an upperclassman made a comment about my hair. Her name is still etched in my memory, but for this narrative, I will refer to her as The Girl. The names of some people you never forget, even forty-plus years later. The Girl said that my hair looked like the ocean. Time stopped for a moment as my brain began processing this comment; then a shudder ran through my body with the realization that I was just verbally assaulted by an upperclassman. A release of adrenaline resulted, but it all went straight to my stomach as

I felt a pit suddenly develop in it. Mentally, I turned in on myself, shrinking internally, feeling anger and embarrassment and distress, all at the same time. I hurt. I was hurt. I wanted to go home, close my bedroom door, and stay there, locked within the security of my room. But, of course, I couldn't.

This was my first experience with being made to feel bad about my appearance, and, worse yet, my first experience with actually *feeling* bad about my appearance due to someone else's comments about me. Everyone has one of these moments. I don't think you can escape your teenage years without one.

An association developed between The Girl's comment about my hair and the shirt that my mom bought for me, the shirt that I really liked and had worn on the day of the assault. I couldn't wear it again. It reminded me of that moment. In fact, I can still visualize the auditorium scene to this day; it is burned into my brain.

* * *

I digressed. Back to the scissor-happy vice president...

So there I am, with only his desk separating me from him, and he is now reaching for scissors. I had a moment of flashback to the feelings that The Girl inflicted upon me the day I felt so great about my appearance my freshman year. It was all in a flash. But then my brain suddenly pushed me to react in a way that my bodily motions and mouth involuntarily followed.

I looked straight into the eyes of my scissor-happy vice president, turned my tie around to reveal the designer label, and calmly said, "It's a Fendi." Scissor Man stopped, looked at my tie, looked up at my face, then pushed back in his seat. He smiled. My brain exploded with, *SCORE!!!!!* Me, the entry-level executive, stopped Mr. Scissors, my vice president, cold.

By this time in my life, I had come to the understanding that how I felt about myself had little to do with what I was wearing or how my hair was behaving. But, still, even for those who have a strong center core within their being, a great-looking suit or other outfit can elevate the day, allowing us to feel as if we are walking on air, about one-half inch off the ground, with heads held a little higher and facial expressions a little happier, arms swinging a little more in rhythm, and the brain saying to itself, *Yeah, I feel good.*

I like wearing suits, but it is not the norm any longer for workplace attire. I still find, though, upon entering meetings or boardrooms, when the room is filled with men and women in professional dress, when pitchers of water and accompanying glasses are on the table instead of plastic bottles of water, when briefs and agendas are neatly arranged in front of each seat, that the atmosphere and the productivity of the meetings tend to be more directed and purposeful. The attendees tend to conduct themselves with a more elevated professionalism. Perhaps those at the table, as the men sit there in their suits and the women in their form of professional attire, have their brains echoing to them, *Sharp. Put together. Yeah, I feel good.*

Silence

I bought my first 35 mm camera in the 1990s. It was a well-researched purchase. I had always wanted one. My parents had a Brownie and took lots of photos in their earlier life. They bought an Instamatic camera for me when I was about twelve years old. It was a Christmas gift, complete with a carrying case. I put it down on the counter at the gift shop of the Ford Theater in Washington, DC, on a tour there with my family and Uncle Andy, Aunt Joanne, and Cousins Andy and Doug. I looked away. In that instant, it was gone. One of the photos on a roll of film that I had taken out of the camera before the theft is of my cousins Andy and Doug, my brother Bob, and me in front of President John F. Kennedy's grave in Arlington National Cemetery. I still have that photo. The memory of my stolen camera resides within it.

It was easy to find film for my new 35 mm camera at my local Duane Reade pharmacy back then, easy, too, to have my film developed there. One day when exiting the Twenty-Eighth Street and Park Avenue subway station on my way home from work, I noticed Photobar as I walked down the left side of Twenty-Eighth Street. I decided to give the shop my next roll of film to develop as a try.

When time came, I met the owner, Sean, who was engaging and quite helpful in my decision process. I decided, *Yep, I will return.* He was a professional photographer, not an associate in a pharmacy who was managing my precious recordings of life.

And I did return many, many times since then. Sean developed too many rolls of film to even begin counting: of family in Black Lick, and Cousin Linda and her kids' visits to New York; the streets and sites of Paris; the canals of Amsterdam and Bruges, Belgium; the ruins of ancient Rome and the beautiful countryside of Orvieto, Italy, where, similar to Frances Mayes, author of *Under the Tuscan Sun*, I would love to live someday; summers on Cape Cod; my time living and working in Florida; and so on.

Sean photographed my business partner, Kim, and me for our professional headshots in his studio. He reproduced countless old black-and-white photos from my parents' photo albums, photos that I wanted to share with my cousins now that our parents are no longer with us in a physical form. And, last year, he composed an incredible collage of photos to give to my cousin Marla as a sixteen-by-twenty-inch gift, photos of her life and family. Sean assisted me in the layout, selecting the frame and matting, and, of course, did the framing. And he packaged and mailed it for me! And Sean, upon buying my first digital camera, showed me the difference in photo quality between 35 mm and digital; digital lacked the depth of 35 mm.

My cousin Diana and I embarked, in 2011, on a mission to record our Bernini family history, starting with our grandparents' lives in Solignano and Berceto, Italy. It has been a labor of love, covering their eight children and their spouses, and their twenty-two grandchildren, our first cousins. Over the past two years, we began to develop the history into written vignettes, sending several pages each month to the cousins for their review, edits, and enhancements. Our hope is to someday publish the family history in book form for posterity.

During this process, Diana and I also began including family photos. We have a ton of black-and-whites from the early 1900s forward, photos from our parents' albums, and photos that our cousins have given to us for this family record. Sean has been more than generous in assisting me in reproducing them to send to our cousins with our written words, as well as image and color correcting them for clarity and vibrancy, since many are fading. Each photo was digitally recorded for our future use. I promised Sean a credit in the book if we ever do get to publish it.

This July, I took another batch of photos to Sean. I asked him how business was for him, given the coronavirus pandemic. New York City had reopened after our long shelter-in-place period. Sean told me that he may need to close his photo studio and shop, as most of his business came from other businesses in the area, work that had ceased with the pandemic. He went on to tell me, though, that he was working with his landlord to try to keep his shop open.

I was shocked, but not shocked, as businesses in my neighborhood in New York City were closing weekly by this time. I was saddened by his news, and certainly wasn't ready to hear it.

Sean's news came on the heels of the closing of Bistango, a favorite neighborhood Italian restaurant. It was impossible to get a table there on a weekend, as it was *the* spot to have Italian. Anthony, the owner, created an environment that made you feel as if you were in an Italian relative's home having dinner. He and his staff would visit each table, often sitting down to chat, and always topping off your glass of wine on the house. I celebrated many birthdays there for friends, including an incredible one for my dear and longtime friend Della, and hosted many of my business's holiday dinners there. It was the place to take out-of-town guests, including Cousins Linda and Barb, who enjoyed conversation with Anthony as much as they enjoyed the food and atmosphere. And my former work colleague Ed often gathered our Liz Claiborne Retail alumni there for reunion dinners. But a phone call from Heron, Bistango's manager, came one day that leveled the news: they were permanently closing. The pandemic. I had been going to Bistango since its opening twenty-five years before.

When I returned to pick up my photos from Sean, he told me that he had to close the business. Thirty years of work. Over. A business privately owned, built from the ground up with his wife, a strong clientele, serving the local community, knowing many of his clients by first name, an effort of love and sweat and long nights in creating a personal success was now closing. He and his wife decided to return to South Korea to assist his aging parents. Sean was putting his studio equipment in storage, hoping to return in one year to assess the environment to reopen or to permanently move on to something else and sell their apartment in New York City.

I rushed back with a bag of old black-and-white photos that I knew Diana and I would need over the next year or so. Sean and I had our usual session of poring over the photos and deciding what to do with them. But, now, it was the last time. Sean had his wife take a photo of the two of us together. He told me that he would be in touch if he reopened. I appreciated his thoughtfulness.

A week later, I returned to pick up his work, my completed photos; after a long conversation, we exchanged pleasantries as I departed. I wished him blessings and wellness. After so many years of walking in and out of his shop, so many years of exchanging stories as we pored over my vacation and family photos together, I was leaving for the last time. I felt numb. Numb for him. Numb for what was happening around me from the ripple effect of the pandemic.

Laura, the hostess at Bistango, was working her way through college. Endrit, a waiter, was from Italy, spoke three languages, and was working part-time at Bistango while he sought an international finance position in the United States. Beautiful Mia, a waitress, was studying Spanish to broaden her communications repertoire, and Domingo, a busboy, always shared his broad smile during my feeble attempts to speak to him in Spanish, probably wondering in the back of his mind what the heck I was trying to say. They, among others, were all now suddenly without the employment that was supporting their dreams, their hopes, their educations.

The decline in small businesses in New York City started before the pandemic. It wasn't due to Amazon, as most may think. It was due to rising rents, which we heard too many times from local business owners. Storefront vacancies grew over the years, but escalated with the effects of the pandemic. While storefronts closed, new construction on luxury, high-rise apartments abounded to the point that a friend in the real estate industry told me that the city was heading for a surplus-inventory position in apartments. It was a recipe similar to the go-go eighties before the financial collapse of 1987. Now, the pandemic complicates the situation.

The brother of my grandmother Bernini, my great-uncle Rudy, and his wife, my great-aunt Rose, raised their young family in the tenement environment of the Lower East Side of Manhattan (think the scenes from Frances Ford Coppola's 1972 movie *The Godfather*) during the 1918 influenza pandemic. New York was hit hard, and I am sure Uncle Rudy and Aunt Rose maneuvered life carefully as they watched friends' and neighbors' lives be affected by the pandemic.

Now, the people who lived through the 1918 pandemic are nameless statistics among sterile but jarring recordings of that time in history books. My friend Maria said yesterday in a phone call with me that the full picture of what we are living through won't be understood in our lifetime. When it is, the history books will record nameless and faceless yet jarring situations and statistics. What they won't know about or fully understand is the effects of the coronavirus pandemic on Sean or Bistango's Anthony, Heron, Endrit, Mia, or Domingo. The lost jobs, the closed stores, the photo-studio equipment in storage, the tossing of the last of your restaurant's twenty-five-year-old interior décor into a dumpster, the sleepless nights, and the gnawing feeling in stomachs as to the loss of a lifetime of personal energies and creativity, of building dreams.

"Sentimental Lady"

I was in Duane Reade today, my local pharmacy, purchasing another box of Band-Aids. I had four boxes of them in my linen closet, not one of which contained the size I needed to cover a new outcropping of eczema after my application of medicine. While perusing an entire shelf of too many options, I found myself suddenly hearing Bob Welch's "Sentimental Lady" playing around me. Muzak. Another song from my college days now playing as background music, elevator music, doctor's office music, and so on.

"Sentimental Lady" is a calming, sensual song. It was played often in the mornings on WDVE in Pittsburgh as I was nursing my first cup of coffee at my dorm-room desk. I am and always was a slow mover in the mornings. I inherited this trait honestly from my parents. WDVE had a female morning DJ at the time. She spoke with a low, sensual voice, often opening her programs with, "This is Marcia in the Morning, here at WDVE." She'd then introduce a song or two. "Sentimental Lady" was a more mellow one. I remember Marcia once opening her 7:00 a.m. show with, "Let's start off the morning with a little Steve Miller Band, 'Fly Like an Eagle.'" It was a great way to start my day. I have already heard "Fly Like an Eagle" in an elevator. I am waiting for the Doobie Brothers' "China Grove" and Elton John's "Rocket Man" to be mellowed down to elevator music. It may have already happened.

These songs once were part of my daily life years ago. Associated with these songs were friends and places and events and feelings and emotions that I felt as now, as present, as happening, as incredibly important, incredibly relevant. I connected with the songs in many ways, and they connected with me.

Now, these songs are associated with friends who remain incredibly important, but the places, events, emotions, etc., are memories, brought forth in elevators, or while waiting in a doctor's office, or when buying Band-Aids in Duane Reade. Memories which elicit knowing smiles. It's funny how this transition happens in life.

Strange People in My Dreams

From where do the people of whom we have no conscious recollection of ever meeting originate in our dreams? Are they strangers that our subconscious registered in our memories of people next to us in a grocery store, on the subway, or in an elevator? Were they passersby on the street or sitting two rows down and three seats over from us in a stadium or theater, people who for a minute caught our eye? Or are they people from another life our souls once lived, now roaming our memories in contemporary clothing and wishing to make contact with us again? I am constantly amazed at the faces and number of people who show up in my dreams who leave me wondering, *Who are these people? Where did I ever meet them? Did I ever meet them?*

I enjoy dreaming about people who are currently in my life. While my mother is no longer physically present on this Earth, I welcome any and all dreams about her. Years ago while I was at a bar during graduate school with a group of friends, one of the women looked at my friend and me and called us, "Mama's Boys." I don't remember the circumstances, but I know it wasn't intended to be malicious. I do remember that neither of us denied it or even replied. Yes, she was right. I was and still am my mother's boy; it is a badge of honor I proudly wear. I like when she appears to me in my dreams. I always feel her presence then and her connection. I often wonder if she is visiting me at those times.

And then there are those people who suddenly surface in my dreams who really are from my past. I often wonder what the trigger is that causes them to surface suddenly. Maybe my subconscious is just opening old boxes of memories and leaving the lid open a little too long, allowing a memory to escape while I sleep? Maybe time really isn't a continuum, as Einstein theorized, and I am zipping in and out of snippets of my life, but just more conscious of it while dreaming?

Last night, I dreamed of Debbie. She was a high school classmate of mine. In the dream, I was taking my seat in a Broadway theater, looked down, and in the seat next to me was Debbie. I exclaimed, "Debbie!" She gave me a big smile as she looked up at me. As I remember Debbie, she had a signature smile that was wide, warm, and inviting—it complemented her pretty features—a type of smile she shared with two other female classmates of mine, Nancy and Deb. Debbie, too, had a twinkle in her eyes that was always present, as did Nancy and Deb. Someone once told me that people with distinctive eye twinkles are new souls, young at heart, lively, curious, and inviting people.

Debbie was one of those girls in my class whose carriage, poise, and grace exhibited a sophistication beyond her years. She was one of our award-winning majorettes performing feats during competitions that, no doubt, astounded the judges, as it did those who were watching from the stands. Soft-spoken, she was one of those fortunate teenagers who never seemed to exhibit stress in school. If it was present, her smile hid it.

In my dream, Debbie continued looking at me from her seat, with her broad, warm smile and eyes twinkling as I sat down next to her. We appeared in ages as if we were back in high school. I remember my surprise upon seeing her and feeling that familiarity we all have when meeting someone from our past, a comfort level that your common backgrounds or experiences ensure easy conversation and no awkward moments of silence.

In her voice, which was still familiar to me, she asked where I now lived.

I replied, "Thirty-Eight and First, near the UN." I asked her where she was living.

She replied in a dream-state voice, a muffled, "Between Chelsea and South Stewart."

I knew in my dream that neither location was an actual address for her and recalled during her answer that I thought she was living somewhere in the Upper Midwest.

Debbie told me in the dream that our high school days were some of the best years of her life. (Where this all came from is beyond my conscious understanding as I type this.)

I remember looking at her; out of courtesy, I was about to agree, but caught myself. For me, my college years were some of the best years of my life, if we were comparing educational experiences. I was about to say this to Debbie, but caught myself again and held back. In my dream, I decided not to say anything that would ruin her warm-memory moment of her high school experiences.

The dream morphed to us sitting beside each other on an airplane. She was in the window seat; I had the aisle. In real life, I prefer aisles, so a little of my reality had crept into this part of the dream. We continued talking. She told me that one of the girls in our class married for money.

Yes. *Where did this all come from?!?!* I asked myself.

But the flight soon ended after that, and we deplaned. In the airport, Debbie looked back over her shoulder at me, her broad smile and her eyes still twinkling as we went our separate ways to places unknown to me as I woke.

So why Debbie and why a Broadway show and why an airplane and why mention a girl who married for money? Was it the hamburger with onions and mustard on a brioche roll and glass of Chianti I had for dinner last night? Was it the Mutsu apple I had for dessert? Was it watching on TCM *Butch Cassidy and the Sundance Kid* after dinner? Whatever and whyever, it was nice to spend a few moments with Debbie again.

Thank you, Debbie, for our reunion. I hope all is well with you and your family and that you arrived safely to your destination, wherever you were going when you stepped off the plane with me.

Weather

I moved to Manhattan after graduate school in 1982. It was a move made out of job desperation, as I was not finding employment for a newly minted MBA in Pittsburgh, the city in which I completed my degree and which, at that time, was still undergoing the metamorphosis from a steel town to something else. The something else wasn't fully defined yet.

After four months in New York City, realizing that I could barely afford to eat, let alone pay Manhattan rents, a fellow Pitt grad and I rented a two-bedroom apartment on Sixth Avenue in the Park Slope section of Brooklyn. Trendy Park Slope. Everyone was moving there, although I didn't know that at the time.

Bernie was our landlord. The apartment was ground floor with a partially finished basement. Amazing. And, being on the ground floor, it had a private yard. Amazing again. A neophyte to New York City and its boroughs, I had no idea what a find this was, and all for six hundred dollars per month. Today, I am sure that rent is now more than ten times that amount.

The unit was called a garden apartment. This was somewhat of a stretch, as the backyard was a jungle of weeds and garbage. After settling into the apartment, I took my Western Pennsylvania gardening talents to that yard. Two weekends and thousands of large garbage bags later, I could see the ground, the fencing which enclosed the yard, and the building behind our apartment. Next job, turning over the soil to plant some yet-unknown greenery.

One week later, after turning over the entire backyard with a shovel I found in the partially finished basement, the apartment was overrun with mice. Yep. Mice. Apparently, while gardening, I'd destroyed a suburbia of mouse homes. Traps later, they were gone, either to another mouse suburbia or disposed of in some other way...except for one...which had passed away in the fluorescent light fixture in our kitchen.

It was a light fixture we didn't like, and I decided to replace it one Saturday afternoon. Electricity turned off and a few screws loosened, I dislodged the fixture from its fifty-some years of existence on that ceiling. As I lowered the fixture, I felt something fall from it, brushing across my face and landing on the floor next to the ladder on which I was standing. It was one of the mice that had passed during the great mouse migration from our backyard.

Let me say it again—it fell, **BRUSHING ACROSS MY FACE**. That was about forty years ago. I am still not right.

My morning routines before leaving for work from that Park Slope apartment always started with a 5:45 a.m. alarm, followed by two cups of coffee at the kitchen table while watching an early morning workout program on the television. After the workout session, I caught the six-o'clock, early-morning news to learn what the weather would be for the day. Then I showered, dressed, packed the briefcase, searched for a subway token, put on outerwear (if it was winter), and off I went to start my day. Exhilarating. Well, some mornings were exhilarating. I am not a morning person.

For years, I listened intently to the television for the weather each morning. This came after watching the eleven-o'clock news the night before to catch their version of the weather for the next day. Later in life, I moved to the ten-o'clock evening news; 11:00 p.m. had suddenly become a little too late.

As a kid back in Western Pennsylvania, WJAC was our local television station out of Johnstown. My hometown of Black Lick was closer to Johnstown than to Pittsburgh, so my parents tended to watch the local news broadcast on WJAC, rather than one of the Pittsburgh stations. I remember well the weathermen on WJAC. They mostly held my undivided interest when snow was predicted for the next day, and all fingers were crossed that roads would be impassable and school would be cancelled. Most of the time, it was wishful thinking that ended with a very disappointed little boy packing his book bag the next morning and trudging through a couple of inches of snow, which was not enough to cancel school. We had book bags back then, not backpacks.

One weatherman on WJAC was a lively man who stood in front of a large board, which may have been covered with an adhesive to which felt would stick. As he spoke, he attached felt cutouts of the sun, moon, rain clouds, snowflakes, and so on to the sticky board. The sun was always a happy sun. I remember that. The weather focus was all local. He didn't report on the West Coast or the Gulf Coast, or even the tri-state area. He focused on Johnstown and its surrounding area. I don't think anyone even cared about the weather for the rest of the country at that point; we were focused on us. He was usually correct, correct enough that people believed him.

Today, I still listen to the weather on the nightly news and again on the morning news. Well, most mornings. My morning routine, almost forty years later, is still pretty consistent. Wake up around 5:45 a.m. and drink two cups of coffee. Watching the morning exercise program on television has been replaced, though, by my obsessive-compulsive need to check my emails, check Facebook, check LinkedIn in my never-ending frenzy to see if I missed something. When done, I sometimes skim the headlines of the *New York Times* online. Skim, because I don't have time to read an entire article since I have so many other very important, very pressing things to see on my laptop screen while rushing through my two cups of coffee.

Too many times now, I look out the windows of my home and wonder if the people reporting on the weather in the mornings have looked out of the windows of their broadcast studio before going on the air. What I see and what I hear seem to be different, too often, and I hear myself loudly exclaiming to the weather person on the TV screen, "Have you looked out the window?"

Perhaps it was the felt cutouts of the moon, sun, snowflakes, and rain clouds that the weatherman on WJAC used years ago that helped better predict the weather. Perhaps, too, they looked out the window before going on-air.

Dr. Herbie

I am home in New York City now, but still doing work for my client in Mexico City. The coronavirus pandemic continues, although our country is beginning to open again while the number of cases increases nationwide. From the windows of my home, I still see the hospital workers at New York University Langone Hospital; they line up each day for health checks before entering their hospital. Down Second Avenue are the freezer trucks at Bellevue Hospital for those deceased whom the funeral homes cannot yet take.

Mexico City is experiencing a crisis similar to that experienced by New York City a few weeks ago; hospital beds and ICUs are filling to capacity, and funeral homes are overrun. We now work via Zoom, as does most of the country. My flights to Mexico were canceled by the airlines weeks ago; the hotel cancelled my reservations as they notified me that they were closed until further notice.

It is interesting how life causes sudden and unexpected intersections for us. My cousin Diana and I have been documenting our Bernini family history for years now, beginning with our grandparents' lives in Berceto and Solignano, Italy. We just completed an initial narrative on our grandmother, although much research is still needed to complete her story. Once again in life, we have many questions on our heritage, and no one still alive to ask.

While going through my mother's photo albums for this project, I came across a photo of Herbie. It was among Mom's collection of photos of her high school friends. Only Herb's name was written on the back, so I don't know if it was his high school or college photo. It is one of those photos, though, for which we all sat at that time in life, thinking we were ready for the world, but not knowing that the world, too, was waiting for us.

Recently, I connected with Herb's daughter, Deb, on Facebook. Deb and I were classmates during our junior and senior high school years. It is interesting how those two occurrences suddenly and randomly overlapped in my life. I remembered Deb well—a very pretty young lady with a warm smile, a calming demeanor, and a member of our senior homecoming court. If my memory serves me, she was also a cheerleader. I do remember clearly, though, that she could have been elected "Class Nicest" if we'd had such a vote.

Herb was a friend of my mom and dad when they were young. I don't know their entire history together, but do remember that my mom often told me that Herb's mother and my grandmother Bernini were friends. Perhaps they connected early on as newly immigrated young ladies living in Blairsville, Pennsylvania; perhaps they knew each other as two young mothers in the 1910s and 1920s, raising families in the town of Black Lick. I heard stories of my parents, Herb, and their friends when they were teenagers and, later, dating stories that made me laugh at the time. But these were stories that belonged to my parents. I only personally remember Herb, though, as my childhood physician, Dr. Herbie.

Mom often reminded me on my birthdays of the events that occurred on the day I was born. Another doctor was my birth doctor. Early on, my lips were suddenly blue. I grew anemic, and with this, Mom and Dad turned to their friend Dr. Herbie for help. I know they had a level of comfort and trust with Dr. Herbie that was foundational from their early, shared lives together.

I wouldn't eat, and when old enough to walk, my older cousins often remind me to this day, of how my mother chased me around the house with a full spoon of food to try to get nourishment into me. Mom often sat me at the kitchen sink to play with running water as a distraction while she fed me. And I do remember gagging on almost everything. The mother of my kindergarten classmate Amy came to our home once with two bottles of child vitamins. One vitamin was green; one was yellow; both tasted like dirt. I gagged as my mom tried to make me swallow one with a glass of water while Amy's mother looked on. It didn't go down. I then took it upon myself to chew it. A sugary, chewy current-day vitamin, it wasn't. It didn't go down. Amy was there. She still remembers the scene to this day.

After that, I started going regularly to Dr. Herbie's office for injections. I think Mom and Dad told me they were vitamin B injections for my anemia. I was old enough to remember those visits to Dr. Herbie's office. He always had a big smile for me as he lifted me onto his examination table. He looked at me directly as he asked me in his gentle, calming voice how I felt. He warmed his ever-present stethoscope before applying it to my skinny little chest and gently prodded my abdomen, making me laugh as he did. Moments such as these, once we are old enough to remember them, never leave us, for some reason. Perhaps it is the kindness of people that remains most vivid in our recollections. Maybe it was the lollipop that I received at the end of the exam that helped.

If I didn't cry in Dr. Herbie's office, Dad took me to G. C. Murphy, down the street from Dr. Herbie's office, to reward me with a toy. It was during one of these noncrying sessions that I got my Beany-Copter cap, a red-plastic cap with a yellow windup copter blade on top. When I pulled on the cord that held the cap on my head, the copter blade would spin off into the air. Dad suggested that I not try this while I sitting next to him in the front seat of our car on the way home that day. My Beany-Copter cap was a marketing tool for one of my favorite cartoons, *Beany and Cecil*, about a little boy and his best friend, a sea serpent. This was way before the bombardment of marketing for children's products that we endure today.

Sometimes when I was sick, Dr. Herbie came to our home on what was then called Church Street in Black Lick; we lived across from the Methodist Church in the yellow, two-story clapboard house. I remember his black bag and the ever-present stethoscope. As a curious kid, I was always wondering about the contents of that bag, trying to peer into it to see what was in there, and often fearful of the potential shot (injection) that it could contain, a shot that may eventually end up in my butt.

Mom and Dad later sold that home to Dr. Herbie's brother and his wife. It was the first home I knew, and my memories of it are still quite vivid: a large home with pocket doors on the first level, a grand staircase with a landing, and a curved hallway on the second floor. It also had a finished room in the attic and a very large, terraced backyard. To this day, I wonder why it had a finished room in the attic and why my parents sold that home and built their 1960s ranch.

A few years ago, I drove by that two-story home. It was in a state of disrepair, with one of the pillars on the front porch missing. That is a memory I wish I didn't have.

Sally was the office manager for Dr. Herbie. Sally was the sister-in-law of my dad's sister Joyce. Aunt Joyce was married to Colonel William Barkley. Sally, like Dr. Herbie, always had a big smile for me as I entered the waiting room of Dr. Herbie's office. She was a family connection in that office, which also contained the early friendship connection of Dr. Herbie to my parents. Connections—and perhaps comfort—all around.

I remember Dr. Herbie's nurse too; her name was Hazel, and she wore a white nurse's uniform, white stockings, and a stiff white nurse's cap. She looked as if she meant business, but was as nice as pie.

The windows of the waiting room in Dr. Herbie's office, on Market Street in Blairsville, were shaded by a yellow, 1960s translucent screen with a design molded into it. The shading had a calming effect on the waiting room, which was filled with mid-century modern furniture.

I was back in Dr. Herbie's office on a regular basis when the anemia returned during puberty. I guess the push and pull of my body's metamorphosing into what it would be for the rest of my life, coupled with evolving mentally into a budding teenager and the stress of surviving junior high school while maintaining my grades, was too much for my system.

During this time, Dr. Herbie became Dr. H. to me. His gentle nature was ever present, but he now spoke to me as an adult regarding my need to personally take care of my health. It was that life-defining moment that we all experience but don't realize it until later—that moment when the umbrella of universal parental dependence and protection begins to close, and we assume ultimate responsibility for ourselves.

Although Dr. H. could no longer lift me onto the examination table, he still warmed the stethoscope before placing it against my scrawny teenage chest. During this time, Mom once pureed raw liver in her efforts to "build up my blood" and curb the anemia problem in me. She secretly mixed it in with my favorite cranberry sauce. I loved it until my godmother, Aunt Nellie, unbeknownst to my mom, tasted it and later told her that it was the best cranberry sauce she ever had. Unfortunately, I overheard the conversation, and that was the last I ate of the medicinal cranberry sauce.

Four years later, I was back in Dr. H's office for the physical required by my college of choice, Saint Vincent

College, in Latrobe, Pennsylvania. It was the same college Dr. H. attended. I remember the visit, and I remember proudly telling him that he was one of the reasons I had chosen Saint Vincent. At the conclusion of the physical, Dr. H. firmly shook my hand, looked me once again in the eyes, and wished me good luck. He smiled his broad, warm smile as he said this.

Yes, it is the kindness of people that we remember. Dr. Herbie has been my benchmark for how I believe physicians should treat people, and I still look for his qualities in the doctors I now encounter in life. I did find him again in Jamie, my first regular preferred care physician here in New York City. Jamie was fresh out of his residency, I was very sick with a flu, and he was recommended to me by my dentist. My first visit was a Dr. H. visit, and I remained with Jamie for many, many years until he moved on to another practice.

During one of my early visits, he asked me to have Dr. H's office send all my records to him. I liked that he was interested in the history of my health. I guess Sally compiled the records and forwarded them to Jamie. On one of my return visits, he showed them to me. As we looked over my childhood records, all written in Dr. H.'s "doctor's scrawl," a flood of memories came back to me.

Jamie said that Dr. H. kept very good records. Of course, he did. Embedded in them was the kindness of a physician tethered only to the well-being of his patients, rooted in the family, friendships, and people of his early life in a small town named Black Lick, and later in another named Blairsville.

"Forever Young"

Last night, as I sat in Alfredo di Roma, the Italian restaurant in the Intercontinental Hotel in Mexico City—and about the only restaurant I frequent here due to acquired food issues I have developed over my lifetime—I heard the song "Forever Young," originally done by Alphaville in 1984, playing in the background. This version, though, was a jazz version. I tapped the Shazam app on my cell phone to identify the artist now doing a song I once loved and discovered the remake was by Berk and The Virtual Band. I admit I really like the new version.

My instinct was to immediately text the link for Berk and The Virtual Band's version to my business partner, Kim. She and I share a love of 1980s and 1990s music, and we both definitely love the original version of this song.

Kim replied, after my text, that she thought the song was too slow.

Kim and I have been friends for forty-plus years. And I have worked with her for almost the same amount of time. We don't always agree. One time, a cabdriver in New York City turned around and said to us, "The way you two are arguing, you must be married." We're not. But there is something about a relationship that has lasted this long that could be misinterpreted as such, especially since Kim and I tend not to be shy about expressing our deep-rooted opinions regarding our work. We need to do so. We are business partners...and friends...since 1982.

After Kim's comment about Berk and The Virtual Band's version of "Forever Young," I texted her the original video of this song by Alphaville. It is haunting. What followed was two and one-half hours of rushing to text each other links to our favorite 1980s and 1990s music videos. It turned out to be a great way to pass a Saturday night while alone in a hotel room.

Passing through our frenzied texting was Toto's "Africa," Men at Work's "Down Under," Nena's "99 Red Balloons," Tears for Fears' "Everybody Wants to Rule the World," Thompson Twins' "Hold Me Now," Midnight Oil's "Beds are Burning," When in Rome's "The Promise," and Spandau Ballet's "True." The list was much longer. The result was a night of reliving memories that emanated from the music associated with the songs. One of my first postings to Kim was Joe Jackson's "Steppin' Out," a song I still love, a CD I still have, and the first song I heard in the cab from the airport after deplaning my nineteen-dollar People's Express flight from Pittsburgh to Newark on my first trip to make New York City my home.

The lyrics and music to "Forever Young" remain with me.

I spoke with a colleague from my days working at Liz Claiborne today. I remember Olivia looking incredible in her navy-blue Armani suit she wore for a presentation to the CEO of Liz. I remember Olivia as she was then; that is,

I still see her as she was at that time in our lives. She hasn't changed in my mind. That was twenty years ago.

I also spoke to a college buddy of mine today. I've known Jim for many more years than I have Kim or Olivia. He was the guy down the hall from my dorm room; he befriended me early in our college days, and we quickly bonded. Jim often came into my room to put Boston's *More than a Feeling* album (now called a vinyl) on my roommate's turntable. It was and still is a favorite song of his. We shared many experiences in college, and they have continued throughout our lives. We are still friends. Today, as I spoke with Jim, I realized that I still picture him as the guy I knew in college. Forever Young.

I realized after my chat with Jim that when I think of my friends, in my mind's eye I continue to see them as the people they were when I first met them. They haven't aged. They haven't changed. As life progresses, I wonder if we ever really identify friends with the age that appears on their driver's license? Does someone stop aging mentally, emotionally, and psychologically for us at the point they first impacted our lives? I think of Olivia as we were in the 1990s. I think of Jim as we were in the 1970s. Kim will always be the same Kim from our first meeting in 1982 when I arrived in New York City. They are Forever Young. Perhaps, too, I am to them.

We Didn't Ask His Name

I started attending daily Mass in the late afternoon several years ago. With the pandemic curtailing my travel, I am able to attend most days. My Roman Catholic roots run deep, with a grandmother who was educated in a convent school in Italy and a grandfather who attended a monastery in Italy before boarding a ship in 1904 to immigrate to America. I remember well sitting at the kitchen table as a very young boy, my mom teaching me, line by line, the Lord's Prayer, until I had it completely memorized. Many, many years later, the words she taught me continue to flow naturally from my lips.

I usually sit on the aisle of the left-back row of the Chapel of the Sacred Hearts of Jesus and Mary. The chapel is a five-minute walk from my home. Karen, a friend of mine who also attends daily Mass, sits across from me in the right-back row on the aisle. We usually exchange light conversation before and after Mass. Karen is Ukrainian. She has had much to speak about lately. She gave me a blue-and-yellow ribbon to pin to my jacket. I wear it daily.

Two weeks ago, I walked into church, and a gentleman was in my seat. My creature-of-habit sense of conformity was thrown off as I was forced to survey the pews for another seat. As I passed the gentleman in my seat, he looked up at me and said hello. I returned the hello, and as I did, I realized he may have been homeless.

This gentleman is not the first homeless person to attend Mass in the late afternoons. Lisa frequents often, but not as consistently as she once did. I, like many, picked up a conversation with her years ago, but never learned her story. She dresses nicely, always wears a hat, and always has a New York University Langone Hospital plastic bracelet around her left wrist and a Langone purple outpatient bag in tow. Some days are more difficult for her than others. She has a warm, inviting smile if you engage her in conversation. She likes to be told that she looks nice. Karen once told me that Lisa spends time in the park across from Thirty-Seventh and FDR Drive on the East River, a park that was wiped out by Hurricane Sandy on October 29, 2012, and is still in need of restoration in 2022. I once was worried when I hadn't seen Lisa at Mass in weeks.

Virginia, the pastoral associate at my church, asked me prior to Lent if I would lead one of the six Lenten reflective sessions after Mass during Wednesdays of Lent this year. I accepted, not knowing what I had just signed up for. Virginia had seven program topics from which to select. I told Virginia, "Just give me what no one else takes." I was assigned the session on sin. Hmmm…

I read the study guide for this subject; it didn't resonate with me. So after several walks, and conversations with my cousins Diana and Phyllis, to contemplate my approach, I decided to focus on reconciliation. For this, I developed the talking points into three forms of prayer: from the mind, from the heart, and from the soul. My friend Karen was a great help with my session, proofing my work and making me confident that the group would be engaged.

For those wondering where this is going, prayers from the mind are those quick prayers we each silently say during a day in response to something currently occurring that grabs our attention. Prayers from the heart are prayers for family and friends in need of prayer; they are love-based. Prayers from the soul are prayers to connect foundationally with the spiritual and to connect with departed parents and family. Prayer from the soul is the deepest form of meditation, taking you inside yourself.

The homeless man was in my pew on a Lenten Wednesday. Kathleen was conducting the series that week; her subject was forgiveness. After Mass, the usual group of us gathered in the assembly space in the back of the church, in which sits an almost life-size marble sculpture of the *Pietà*. Kathleen started the session as the homeless man rose from his seat and walked over to one of the *Stations of the Cross* sculptures hanging on the chapel walls.

He seemed to be in prayer. He then paced the back of the church and later came among us to look at another Station sculpture that was behind where we were seated. Then, turning around after a moment of silence, he looked at us and said, "I just want to look at this. I'm sixty-two."

The session stopped. We all looked at him. His kind eyes looked back at us. Kathleen asked him if he would like to join our group that evening. He told us he was Catholic. He accepted.

The homeless gentleman sat between Karen and the *Pietà*. Kathleen handed him a program. At that point in the evening, we were reading the Gospel of John 10:31–42. Each week, we went around the circle of seats, and each person read a line or two of the assigned Gospel until it had all been read. When Karen finished her portion, it was the homeless man's turn to read. Kathleen asked him gently if he would like to read the next line.

The gentleman accepted, and if I remember correctly, he read, "If I am not doing the works of My Father, then do not believe Me" (John 10:37, English Standard Version).

The gentleman continued with our group. Karen's session that evening included sampling of the aromas from the balms referenced in the Bible, the ones used to anoint Jesus's body after his death. The gentleman was intrigued, as we all were.

As we departed that evening, Kathleen, Karen, and I were the last to leave the church. The gentleman was still there. Kathleen and I both explained to him that we needed to close the church, but the gentleman asked to stay for a moment. He then went over to the hanging sculpture of the *Eighth Station of the Cross*, which represents Jesus consoling the women of Jerusalem as He made His way to Golgotha, where He knew He was to be crucified.

The gentleman raised his right hand and touched the *Eighth Station*. In the version of the "Stations of the Cross" booklet that I use, one of the lines to contemplate at this Station is a quote from Jesus:

I comfort those who seek to solace Me.
How gentle can you be, My other self? How Kind?

(Clarence Enzler, "Everyman's Way of the Cross"
[Notre Dame, Indiana: Ave Maria Press, 1970])

The gentleman joined us as we all walked out together and closed the doors to the church behind us.

The next evening at Mass, I asked Karen if anyone asked the gentleman for his name. Neither she nor I remembered asking. We both realized then that this homeless gentleman, who'd spent an hour participating with us during a Lenten reflective session, had departed nameless.

We didn't ask his name.

Leaving Mexico City

On March 9. 2020, I arrived for my last time in Mexico City to work on the project for which I was engaged by El Palacio de Hierro. As usual, my flight came into Aeropuerto Internacional Benito Juárez, and I deplaned, heading with the other passengers to Customs.

By now, I had flown Delta and its affiliate AeroMexico so often that I was being upgraded on my flights to and from Mexico City. This time however, I departed JFK Airport in New York City with disinfectant wipes in a plastic bag and extra bottles of hand sanitizer. This time, too, I gingerly wiped down my entire business-class seat area with the disinfectant wipes. This activity would be repeated again on all surfaces of my hotel room upon arrival.

The trip to my hotel, the Intercontinental, had nothing unusual about it. But for me, I was troubled by the knowledge that I had just departed my home in the Unites States with the understanding that a virus was spreading and that it was dangerous. We were still early on in the pandemic that was to be labeled for the name of the virus, COVID-19. I didn't get the sense that people I was encountering in Mexico City were carrying the same fears, perhaps dread, that I had.

I made sure not to shake hands with anyone, as our governor had warned about this before I departed the United States. The Mexican people are very congenial, and I was accustomed by now to hardy handshakes and warm hugs, and even a few kisses on my cheeks by many of the hotel staff with whom I frequently interacted. I refrained from all of this. Some people had already heard the news about the virus in the United States and understood. To others, I am sure I was acting strangely.

A similar experience occurred my first morning in the offices at Palacio. The project manager with whom I did most of my work was a little put off by my refusal of the usual morning handshake accompanied by a grand hug that, for men, included a shoulder bump. But I wasn't taking any risks.

Fast forward through the week of no personal contact, and the weekend brought news in the hotel that Mexico City was locking down. I raced to change my flight and was able to depart the following Tuesday. By then, the hotel was nearly empty. So was the airport, an airport that rivaled any major one in the United States for crowded corridors of vacationers and the hustling of business men and women to board flights.

I wiped down my seat area again. So did many others. The aroma of disinfectant was prevalent. People used tissues to touch the door handles of the bathroom. I know. I was one of them. I just wanted to get home; the flight couldn't be over fast enough for me.

JFK was nearly empty on my arrival. The screen at the Customs kiosk presented a moment of fear: I had to touch it to gain entry back into the United States. I was equally cautious on my cab ride home from the airport. None of us knew at that point what would happen next.

Wine Delivery

Yesterday, I stopped by Windsor Wines, on Third Avenue between Thirty-First and Thirty-Second Streets, to buy a case of wine. I have been a patron of Windsor Wines for too many years to count; I know one of the managers, Knute, a professional wine expert who is the same age as I. We spend lots of time talking when I am in his shop.

As usual, I asked for my selected case of wine to be delivered. Later, the house phone rang in my apartment, and I was told a delivery was on its way up in the elevator; it was one of two deliveries I was expecting yesterday—Staples and Windsor Wines. By the time I reached the door, the doorbell had chimed, and when I opened the door, there stood the wine-delivery gentleman, the same mid-thirtyish young man—a little shorter than I, with an oval face and black, cropped hair—who has delivered many cases of wine to my home.

He was wearing a blue face mask, and I quickly realized I was not wearing mine. I felt a little naked, a new feeling many of us probably now have when encountering people and realizing we are maskless. We exchanged the usual "How are you doings," and he asked me if I wanted the case brought into the apartment and placed in the front hallway. As he did so, he kept his social distance from me.

I find it interesting and greatly appreciate how others now do the same dance of social distancing that I do.

As the young man turned to leave, something inside of me made me ask him again how he was doing. But, this time, I went further and asked about his family.

He hesitated with his answer, while looking at me with eyes that suddenly spoke volumes. From behind his blue mask, I heard, "My wife died three weeks ago."

The feeling we all experience—the world stopping its rotation for just a second when we receive news we did not expect—hit me. I then said, "I am so sorry." And then, out of my mouth came a question that, only now, any of us could ask, "Was it COVID?"

Again, the world stopped its rotation for me as I realized what I just did. I grew up with, and still have within me, that Western Pennsylvania sensibility that teaches us not to ask questions that pry, to be sensitive, and to respect the privacy of others. With my Italian roots on my mom's side, this sensibility was heightened with lifelong training that we don't talk about the family outside of the family.

From somewhere, once again, I heard my mom say, "What's the matter with you? We don't ask questions like that. Some things are best left unsaid."

But the question was posed, and the young man told me that it wasn't COVID, that his wife had been ill for three years.

I expressed my sympathies again, again inquired as to how he was doing, and told him I would say a prayer for him.

From behind his blue mask, he answered me humbly, his eyes doing more speaking than what came from behind the blue mask.

After he departed, I wondered what his name was. I had never asked. I wondered if he and his wife had children and how the children were doing. He is a delivery man, and I wondered about the funeral costs, which is truly none of my business to even consider. I wondered if he could have a funeral at all, given COVID restrictions. I wondered how he would now manage if he did have children. And I wondered if he was able to be with his wife at those last moments, to hold her hand and kiss her one more time.

In this age of COVID, these are thoughts we may have never entertained prior to 2020. I have no answers, only the sight of him and his eyes and the blue mask from which his message emerged. A space opened in my heart at that moment for this man who is not a stranger to me, but whom I also do not know.

On a flight back from Florida several years ago, a five-year-old British lad sat in the middle seat next to my aisle seat. Smiling broadly, he introduced himself as Henry, while exhibiting a large gap where his two upper front teeth had once resided. His maternal grandparents and eight-year-old sister, Julie, were in the row behind me. His grandmother leaned forward and asked if I minded that

Henry sat next to me. I told her not to worry and that if he needed help, I was happy to give it.

When the flight attendant came by with drinks, Henry asked for white tea. Neither the flight attendant nor I knew what white tea was, but Henry was quick to point out with his English accent, "Put one-half hot water and one-half milk into the cup. Then dip the tea bag into the cup only once." He smiled. The flight attendant smiled. I smiled. The white tea was delivered.

Later, Henry's grandmother passed him a sandwich that she'd bought at the airport. The American-sized sandwich, overwrapped and tightly secured in plastic, was a challenge for Henry to open. He held it up and, covering his face with it, said to Mark in the window seat, "Look. It's as big as my face." Sadly, it was. Henry didn't like it.

My business partner, Kim, refers to airport sandwiches as salt sandwiches. If your fingers and feet don't swell on a flight, then they are guaranteed to do so if you consume an airport sandwich. Or a hot dog.

Still later, when the snacks came around, Henry asked for a biscuit. The flight attendant explained that she didn't have biscuits, but instead handed him a favorite of mine as a kid—a vanilla-cream cookie packet. Same thing, different country. Henry didn't like these either.

As he pushed them away, I recalled my consulting work with a European-based candy company. I was told that they put more sugar in candy to be sold in the United States since we tend to like our candies and desserts sweeter than the Europeans do.

While deplaning, Henry's grandmother thanked Mark and me for taking care of Henry. She then told us that she and her husband had treated their grandchildren with a trip to Disneyworld. And then in a whisper, out of earshot of Henry and his sister, she told us Henry's teeth were knocked out when his father punched five-year-old Henry in the face and rendered him unconscious. Henry remembered nothing of the incident. Grandmother went on to explain the father was now, thankfully, out of the picture. Little Henry. Sandwich-as-big-as-my-face Henry. White-tea Henry. He fell asleep with his head on my shoulder halfway through the flight while watching a cartoon on the seat screen.

I had questions about Henry and his sister, but my Western Pennsylvania sensibilities blocked me from asking them. The world stopped its rotation again for me at that moment. Too painful. Too personal. They were answers I did not need to know, or that others did not need to share with me, as they belonged only to Henry, his sister, Julie, and their grandparents.

I have not been able to forget Henry. Or the eight-year-old young lady and her toddler brother asking for money on the Paseo de la Reforma in Mexico City, about whom I wrote on March 11, 2018. And now, I will not forget about my wine-delivery gentleman. I don't want to forget about them, and I will work to keep them in my memory throughout my life.

These chance encounters with strangers who are there for just a moment in our lives, with whom our souls exchange an energy, with whom a thread forms and never breaks—I believe they are presented to us for a reason. They are gifts that bring us to a more sensitive place of our humanity and our connections to each other. They are there for a purpose, and it is up to each of us to take the time to understand why.

Of Interest about This Work: Mexico City

I am a retail consultant. I've had the good fortune of having a lot of great clients over the twenty years I've been doing this work, and really great travel, most of the time. My area of expertise is more on the side of finance than it is on merchandising, so I don't go to Paris fashion shows, as many people believe the retail industry routinely frequent, well at least those in apparel retailing.

In the fall of 2017, I was engaged by the CEO of Mexico's largest luxury department store, El Palacio de Hierro, to assist the company in a retail-system implementation. I knew the CEO from work I did for a company in Madrid, with which he was once affiliated. I was happy to reconnect with him for this project. Once the due diligence was completed, my business partner, Kim, and I commenced work in January 2018.

The project required me to be on-site every month for two consecutive weeks. We were in a hurry to complete the implementation. Like most system implementations, you never know what you are getting yourself into until you "lift the hood." Twenty-seven months later, after spending two weeks (and sometimes three weeks) each month on-site in the offices of Palacio in Mexico City, I was on an AeroMexico flight home, rushing to leave the city as it began locking down due to COVID-19. The project, by then, was almost complete.

I knew nothing about Mexico City before I arrived for the first time at Aeropuerto Internacional Benito Juárez. Nor had I ever been to Mexico. As the sun came up over the city my first morning there, and as I boarded a taxi to go to the offices of my new client, I was amazed at the beauty and congeniality that were all around me. I could not speak the language, but that didn't seem to matter. Everywhere I went, I was welcomed.

Within the first few months of work, my client moved their offices to the Polanco neighborhood, known for its luxury shopping and international restaurants that sit along Avenida Presidente Masaryk, considered the most expensive street in Mexico. Palacio's new offices were in the office tower above its newly opened flagship store in Polanco. To me, this store is the most beautiful store I have ever experienced. I often said it was the most beautiful store in the Western Hemisphere.

I enjoyed my work. I enjoyed working again with the CEO. I enjoyed meeting his team and working with them. I enjoyed the system's vendor teams brought in from Ireland, Germany, the United States, and, of course, Mexico, with whom I worked. I think I made a few friends for life.

But I also worked really hard as the project grew in scope and complexity. During the weekends that bridged my weeks there, I often just relaxed in my hotel room, reading and catching up on work from the week or working on projects for other clients back in the States. I found myself one early weekend needing—yes, needing— to record a sighting I had, on Paseo de la Reforma, of two small children. Later, I found myself needing again to record an interaction with a barista, which just astounded me, taking me by surprise one day. And thus began my writings herein.

References, Sources, Bibliography

Words

Ehrmann, Max. "Desiderata." 1927.

Millennials

The New Seekers. "I'd Like to Teach the World to Sing." *New Colours*, Metromedia. 1971.

Chance Meetings?

Keys, Alicia. "We are Here" (single). RCA, 2014.

Liza

Paint the Sky with Stars, the Best of Enya. WEA. 1997.

Enya. "Orinoco Flow." Watermark, WEA (Europe), 1988. Watermark, Geffen (US), 1989.

School

The Sting. George Roy Hill, Universal Pictures, 1973.

My Little Margie. Henry King. Twentieth Century-Fox Film
Corporation, 1946.

Dylan, Bob. "Blowing in the Wind" (single). Columbia, 1963.

The Poseidon Adventure. Ronald Neame. Twentieth
Century-Fox Film Corporation, 1972.

John Lennon, Paul McCartney. "When I'm Sixty-Four." *Sgt.
Pepper's Lonely Hearts Club Band,* Partophone, 1967.

Rita

Ledbetter, Huddie (Lead Belly). "Goodnight, Irene."
Melodisc, 1933.

Collections

Knowles, John, *A Separate Peace,* Secker & Warburg, 1959.

Fitzgerald, F. Scott, *The Great Gatsby*, Charles Scribner's
Sons, 1925.

Rand, Ayn, *The Fountainhead,* Bobbs-Merrill, 1943.

Jet Engines

Moore, Clemente Clark. "A Visit from St. Nicholas." 1873.

Dr. Strangelove. Stanley Kubrick. Columbia Pictures, 1964.

Vitamin D and Volcanoes

McGovern, Maureen. *"The Morning After."* The Morning
After, Twentieth Century, 1973.

Doug

Hammer, Ronald and Parker, Phil. *Calamity Jane (A Musical Western),* Directed by Casa Manana, Casa Manana Theater, Fort Worth, Texas, 1961.

Klemmer, John. "Touch." *Touch,* ABC Records, 1975.

Cats

Cats. Tom Hopper. Universal Pictures, 2020.

Webber, Andrew Lloyd. *Cats.* Directed by Trevor Nunn, New London Theater, West End, London, England, 1981.

Eight is Enough. Book by Tom Braden, Developed by William Blinn for ABC, 1977.

Hudson, Jennifer. "Memory." Andrew Lloyd Webber, 1981.

Memories Not Spoken

Dragon, Daryl (Captain) and Tennille, Toni. "Muskrat Love." *Song of Joy,* A&M Records, 1976.

Clapton, Eric. "I Shot the Sheriff." 461 Ocean Boulevard, RSO, 1974.

Silence

Mayes, Frances, *Under the Tuscan Sun,* Chronicle Books, 1996.

The Godfather. Francis Ford Coppola. Paramount Pictures, 1972.

"Sentimental Lady"

Welsh, Bob. "Sentimental Lady." *French Kiss*, Capitol Records, 1977.

Steve Miller Band. "Fly Like an Eagle." *Fly Like an Eagle*, Capitol Records, 1976.

The Doobie Brothers. "China Grove" (single). Warner Brother Records, 1972.

John, Elton. "Rocket Man." *Honky Chateau*, Uni (US) and DJM (UK), 1972.

Strange People in My Dreams

Butch Cassidy and the Sundance Kid. George Roy Hill. Twentieth Century Fox, 1969.

Dr. Herbie

Clampett, Bob. *The Beany and Cecil Show*. Cartoon. American Broadcasting Company, 1959–1962.

Forever Young

Alphaville. "Forever Young." *Forever Young*, WEA, 1984.

Toto. "Africa." *Toto IV*, Columbia, 1982.

Men at Work. "Down Under." *Business as Usual*, Columbia, 1981.

Nena. "99 Red Balloons." *Nena, and 99 Luftballons*, Epic, 1983, 1984.

Tears for Fears. "Everybody Wants to Rule the World." *Songs from the Big Chair*, Phonogram-Mercury-Vertigo, 1985.

Thompson Twins. "Hold Me Now." *Into the Gap*, Arista, 1983.

Midnight Oil. "Beds are Burning." *Diesel and Dust*, Columbia, 1987.

When in Rome. "The Promise." *When in Rome*, Virgin, 1987.

Spandau Ballet. "True." *True*, Chrysalis, 1983.

Jackson, Joe. "Steppin' Out." *Night and Day*, A&M, 1982.

Boston. "More Than a Feeling." *Boston*, Epic, 1976.

Printed in the USA
CPSIA information can be obtained
at www.ICGtesting.com
LVHW021559131023
760998LV00025B/277

9 781637 654101